TRIBUTES

IN LOVING MEMORY OF
Olof and Kristina Erickson, early and generous contributors to the founding of Minnehaha Academy; Mabel Erickson '15 Larson, their daughter, a student the very first year the school opened its doors; Richard E. (attended in '39) and Marion Larson '43 Stromberg, daughter of David and Mabel Larson

GIVEN BY FAMILY MEMBERS
Elwood (Woody) '47 and Janet Valine '46 Larson, Vern '49 and Ruth Larson, Dan and Julie Stromberg '67 Tutt, Teri Stromberg '70 Oelschlager, Mark '74 and Terri Danielson '78 Stromberg

IN HONOR OF
Helen Nordquist '14 Benson, Alpha Nordquist '16 Rasmuson, Greta Thompson '88 Schramm, Scott Thompson '90

GIVEN BY
Helen Benson's daughters: Beverly and Wayne Thompson, Marilyn Brink, LaVonne Sauter, Bernetta Huber

IN MEMORY OF
Arlene Anderson, Minnehaha Academy teacher, dean of students, dean of instruction, and founding principal of the middle school from 1945 to 1984

GIVEN BY
David '67 and Jeanne Anderson (son and daughter-in-law), Jason and Courtney Anderson '99 DaCosta (grandson-in-law and granddaughter)

IN MEMORY OF
Rev. Carl A. Hognander, MA voice instructor, 1913–1916; Orville C. Hognander '31; Marjorie H. Silvis '36; Ann Marie H. Olmstead '40

GIVEN BY
O. C. (Joe) Hognander, Jr.

IN HONOR OF
Our parents, Mark Nelson '54 and Sherrill Anderson Nelson '56

GIVEN BY THEIR CHILDREN
Todd Nelson '79 and Beth Koepp Griggs Nelson '79, Linda Nelson Lehman '82 and David Lehman, Jill Nelson Chelgren '85, Sara Nelson Peterson '90 and Scott Peterson

IN HONOR OF
Our parents, Dave and Mary Jo, Bob and Elaine, Randy and Lori, Ron and Carla, who sacrificed in order for us to benefit from our Minnehaha Academy education

WITH GRATITUDE
Randy Monson '79, Ron Monson '81, Carla Holman '81 Monson, Jennifer Monson '84 Gimpl, Kirsten Monson '07, Cory Monson '08, Britta Monson '09

IN MEMORY OF
Gust E. and Clara M. Ericson

GIVEN BY
Rev. Paul A. Johnson and Barbara Ericson Johnson and their five children: Jeffrey P. Johnson, Joel E. Johnson '77, Lance Johnson, Julie Johnson Peterson '76, Timothy Johnson '81; and their spouses and grandchildren: Jenna E. Johnson '05, John C. Peterson '05, Lindsay E. Johnson '06, Lauren C. Peterson '07, Annelisse K. Johnson '08, Jesse K. Johnson '13

IN MEMORY OF
Lloyd and Gladys Chellin, faithful supporters of the Covenant Church and Minnehaha Academy

GIVEN BY THEIR FAMILY
Betty Chellin '47 Anderson (daughter), Bonnie Anderson (granddaughter), Sashi Anderson '06 Smith (great granddaughter)

IN HONOR OF
The Minnehaha Academy faculty who touched the lives of students from our extended family: Amy Bragg Carey '80, Anna Carey '09, Brett Carey; Rogene Nelson Bragg '52, Mark Bragg '87, Jeff Bragg '89; Richard Holte '45, Leonard Holte '46, Wayne Holte '49, Sarah Holte '86; Molly Larson Bragg '89; Beth Bragg Tastad '87. Thanks also for the opportunity given to brother Dick Bragg and Bill Holte to serve on the faculty

WITH GRATITUDE
James Bragg '49 and Barbara Holte Bragg '53

THESE TRIBUTES ARE PUBLISHED IN GENEROUS SUPPORT OF THIS VOLUME.

Minnehaha Academy
A CENTURY OF FAITH AND LEARNING

"Jesus Christ is the same yesterday and today and forever."
Hebrews 13:8

Minnehaha Academy—that which began as the dream of immigrants—now carries one hundred years of history as a vibrant institution. In that century, thousands of students have come in and gone out of its doors. For all of us, MA is the repository of our memories of the time and effort it takes to cease being a child and begin being an adult. Nostalgia for that time and MA's contribution to our coming of age is natural and proper. This book commemorates the memories that MA holds within its walls. Our school's centennial is a fitting occasion to consider and honor them. Nostalgia, though, implies looking only back. If that is all we do, we might easily miss the most important of MA's many distinctions. It has been, is now, and forever will be a mission—a mission to challenge every student to come face-to-face with the claims of Jesus Christ, to encourage them freely and honestly to consider those claims, and, by so doing, to make faith a natural part of their lives.

Centennial Chairs: David Anderson '67, Jeanne Anderson, Courtney (Anderson) DaCosta '99

COPYRIGHT © 2012 BY MINNEHAHA ACADEMY

3100 West River Parkway
Minneapolis, Minnesota, 55406

All rights reserved, including the right to reproduce this work in any form whatsoever without permission in writing from the publisher, except for brief passages in connection with a review. For information, please write:

THE
DONNING COMPANY
PUBLISHERS

The Donning Company Publishers
184 Business Park Drive, Suite 206
Virginia Beach, VA 23462

Steve Mull, General Manager
Barbara Buchanan, Office Manager
Heather L. Floyd, Editor
Amanda Dawn Guilmain, Graphic Designer
Priscilla Odango, Imaging Artist
Katie Gardner, Project Research Coordinator
Tonya Washam, Marketing Specialist
Pamela Engelhard, Marketing Advisor

Barry Haire, Project Director

Cataloging-in-Publication Data

Minnehaha Academy : a century of faith and learning.
　　p. cm.
 Includes bibliographical references and index.
 ISBN 978-1-57864-517-6 (hardcover : alk. paper)
 1. Minnehaha Academy (Minneapolis, Minn.)--History. 2. Church schools--Minnesota--Minneapolis--History.
 LD7501.M473 .M56
 371.07109776579--dc23
　　　　　　　　　　2012018230

Printed in the United States of America at Walsworth Publishing Company

Table of Contents

6	Foreword
7	Acknowledgments
8	Swedish Roots: 1884–1913
14	*Welcome to Minnehaha Academy*
16	1913–1919
24	*A Christian School*
26	1920–1929
34	*Marks Through the Years*
36	1930–1939
44	*Funds 'n' Friends*
46	1940–1949
54	*Traditions in Transition*
56	1950–1959
64	*Bricks and Bones*
66	1960–1969
74	*Foundation of Faith*
76	1970–1979
84	*Tools of Technology*
86	1980–1989
94	*A New Identity*
96	1990–1999
104	*Kids in the Classrooms*
106	2000–2012
114	*Farewell from Minnehaha Academy*
116	Future Legacy: 2013–
124	One Hundred Years at MA
126	Index
128	Bibliography

Foreword

What becomes of a nascent vision fueled by sacrifice, determination, and God's bountiful blessings and providence? It is the enduring ministry of Minnehaha Academy to generations of gifted young men and women, the surrounding community, the nation, and the world. Struggling for its first life-giving breath in the fall of 1913, Minnehaha, already having committed this vision to fervent prayer, humbly yet boldly laid its foundation along the banks of the Mississippi River and sought to make its presence and mission known. The immense task of starting a school was not the work of one individual, but the united effort of numerous individuals who desired to build a school whose spirit and essence was "Youth Meeting Truth."

The mission to provide high-quality education integrating Christian faith and learning has been honored for a century. A rigorous training of the mind and a commitment to spiritual formation through the academic subjects, the arts, and athletics and the relationship between students and strong Christian role models, their teachers, are the eternal values that Minnehaha brings.

During the past ten decades, the spirit of Minnehaha has been reflected in its people, its tenacity, its God-honoring heritage, and its strong sense of community. The level of passion that unabashedly flows from the lips of those who have served and been educated within Minnehaha's walls has deep and winding roots. The roots have been nourished from a deep sense of love and pride and a commitment to hold fast to our mission and our Christian distinctives in times of despair and drought and in times of great harvest.

Like metamorphic rock that transforms due to intense heat and pressure, we have remained, strong, distinctive, and laden with character. We have been a school that has welcomed first the Swedish immigrants and now those of other cultures, ethnicities, and socio-economic backgrounds. We have welcomed students who showed great academic promise and those who struggled; students who entered with a positive self-image and those who needed to hear they mattered; students whose Christian faith was strong and those who made the life-changing discovery of Christ after admission. The legacy of Minnehaha is revealed through the lives of students where in every sphere they are indispensable members of society.

As Hebrews 13:8 affirms, Jesus Christ is the same yesterday, today, and forevermore. God's vision planted in the hearts of so many is always bigger than our human abilities and thus, we have trusted in him and he has been our guide. To God we owe a great debt of gratitude for the stories and events that the pages of this work unfold. It is a cause for great celebration!

Donna M. Harris
President

Acknowledgments

This book would not have been possible without the tireless efforts of the members of the Centennial History Committee who helped organize the Alumni/Archive House, assist with research, share their memories, and provide editorial guidance on the book. Special thanks to Jim Nash for volunteering his time and expertise to take photographs of original archival materials. Thanks to Curt Bjorlin and Jim Wald who, directly or indirectly, provided the muscle to get all the archival materials from scattered locations around the campus over to the house. Thanks also to editor Heather Floyd and graphic designer Amanda Guilmain and Stephanie Danko for their expertise and guidance which ensured the professional quality of this book.

A special thanks goes to Gerald Nordstrom, whose previously published book, *Where Youth Meets Truth: A History of Minnehaha Academy*, served as an immense resource for research and inspiration and spared countless hours of work thanks to his efforts. The prior publication of *Where Youth Meets Truth: A History of Minnehaha Academy* as a detailed history of the school has allowed this book to adopt a more flexible approach. The purpose of this book is not to be comprehensive, but rather to celebrate a century of faith and learning. Anyone interested in further information about any of the events or people mentioned are encouraged to read through Nordstrom's book, still available from the school; to visit the Minnehaha Academy website (MinnehahaAcademy.net); and to stop by and browse through Minnehaha Academy's newly established Alumni/Archive House, which now stores all the school's archival materials, including all past yearbooks, school newspapers and publications, photos, videos, buttons, trophies, and much more.

In addition to photo credits, a special thanks is extended to the following organizations and individuals who have provided the school and subsequently this book with expert photography:

Dell Larson Studios
H. Larson Studios/Dave Santos
Dave Olsen Photography, Inc.
Saving Tape Media Conversion and Thor Anderson
Ake G. Lundberg
Jim Nash
Audrey Bergengren

Carrie Johnson
Pauline Ojambo
Reid Westram
Laurie Pease Johnson
Elaine Ekstedt
Bonnie Addington
Mark Norlander

A BRIEF NOTE TO THE READER

The author of this book wishes to express to the reader a knowing awareness that too much of the school's history is truncated, due to the brevity of this volume, for every important event, sport, individual, memory, etc. to be properly honored. The author also wishes to acknowledge that, while every effort has been made to ensure the factual accuracy of the information continued herein, those efforts are still human at best. Therefore, if for any reason there are those who are offended by certain omissions or errors, glaring or otherwise, the author wishes to express sincerest apologies and, believing that humor is fair medicine for effrontery, share with the reader an excerpt from the 1927 *Antler*:

> This book's a great invention,
> The school gets all the fame.
> The Printer gets all the money,
> The Staff gets all the blame.

Swedish Roots: 1884–1913
THE IDEA FOR A SCHOOL

Minnehaha Academy opened its doors to the first school day of its first school year on the banks of the Mississippi River on Monday, September 15, 1913. The Centennial celebration recognizes the one hundred years that the school has kept those doors open from 1913 to 2013. However, before there were classes, before there was a school building, before there was even land on which to build a school, Minnehaha Academy existed as an idea. The work of the many people who turned that idea into a reality is the story of what took place before the first day of school in 1913.

SWEDISH ROOTS

Reverend Erik August Skogsbergh was one of the greatest motivating forces behind the idea for Minnehaha Academy. E. A. Skogsbergh was born in Varmland, Sweden, in June 1850. He arrived in the United States from Sweden in 1876. He first began preaching in America in Chicago's North Side Mission Church on Franklin Street. Skogsbergh's increasing popularity and expanding congregations led to the construction of his first Swedish Tabernacle in Chicago, which would become the site where, in 1885, the denomination now known as the Evangelical Covenant Church of America took form. Skogsbergh's preaching was also in demand in Swedish-speaking communities beyond Chicago, including Minneapolis and St. Paul. During his first visit to Minneapolis in 1877, he repeatedly filled the city's largest halls.

E. A. Skogsbergh.

Skogsbergh answered a call to serve a congregation in Minneapolis in 1884. He built the second of his Swedish Tabernacles in 1886. Skogsbergh's third Swedish Tabernacle would be constructed in Seattle, Washington. In addition to his preaching, he helped form the Swedish Christian Mission Association of the Northwest, originated the Swedish-language publication *Veckobladet* ("The Week's News"), and was a leader in founding the Swedish Hospital in Minneapolis. From his arrival in America, Skogsbergh also recognized the need to provide education and training opportunities for fellow immigrants, so he began a school that would meet this need.

(Photo reproduction courtesy of Jim Nash)

Veckobladet began as a religious weekly first published by Skogsbergh's Minneapolis Veckoblad Publishing Company in 1884. The name of the paper was changed to *Minneapolis Veckoblad* in 1887, and the name *Veckobladet* was finally adopted in 1906 "in order to imply a more national and less regional character" (P. Anderson 1984, 38).

(Photo courtesy of Jim Nash)

8 Minnehaha Academy: A Century of Faith and Learning

SKOGSBERGH'S SCHOOLS

In the fall of 1884, Skogsbergh started The Minneapolis Business School and Bible Institute, his first school, which provided employment education and Biblical studies for Swedish immigrants. Starting with just nineteen students, the school met in Skogsbergh's own home, but as enrollment grew, the school relocated twice before settling into the lower level of the Swedish Tabernacle in Minneapolis. In addition to teaching general coursework in English, American history, and geography, Skogsbergh's school also taught music, business, and Bible, as well as courses in Swedish language and culture. The school operated for seven years before being given over to the Covenant denomination as a gift in 1891.

In the fall of 1891, the school, now belonging to the Covenant denomination, opened with three teachers: David Nyvall, seminary teacher and acting president; J. A. Lindblade, teacher for the Commercial Department; and A. L. Skoog, who taught English part time. As the Covenant school continued to grow, the limited space of the Swedish Tabernacle created the need for an independent school building. While Skogsbergh proposed a suitable location in Camden Place, five miles north of Minneapolis, the Swedish University Association proposed another location in an undeveloped area north of Chicago. The Covenant elected to move the school to Chicago, where it was established as The Covenant College and Theological Seminary and later became North Park University and Theological Seminary. David Nyvall served as the first president of North Park.

Immediately following this move, Skogsbergh started another school, the Northwestern Collegiate and Business Institute, in 1894. This school began in the vacated space of the Swedish Tabernacle, but increasing enrollment required its relocation in 1902 to a large house. In 1905, the school returned to the Swedish Tabernacle, where it remained until 1911. The creation of this school was the first major step in the official formation of Minnehaha Academy.

Skogsbergh's Svenska Missions Tabernaklet is now known as First Covenant Church, Minneapolis.

An early pamphlet shows the name "Minnehaha Academy," in use before the school was built along the river.

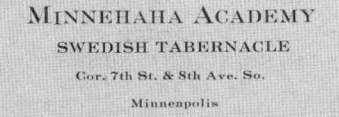

(Photo courtesy of First Covenant Church, Minneapolis archives)

MINNEHAHA ACADEMY
SWEDISH TABERNACLE
Cor. 7th St. & 8th Ave. So.
Minneapolis

Board of Directors:
Rev. A. E. Palmquist, Chairman
Rev. C. G. Ellström, V. Chairman
Prof. D. F. Swenson, Sec'y.
Aaron Carlson, Treas.
Rev. F. O. Kling
Chas. Wallblom
Andrew Nordström

Teachers:
K. E. Forsell   Albert Walin
J. J. Laurell

(Image from the MA archives)

SWEDISH ROOTS: 1884–1913

(Photo and image from the MA archives)

A NAME AND A PLACE
A 1914 photo of the River Road in Minneapolis and a promotional map of the school grounds illustrate how rural the area was at the time in comparison to today.

The supporters of Skogsbergh's second school recognized the need for an independent building. In 1904, a tract of twenty-eight acres along the banks of the Mississippi River was found and determined to be an ideal site for the school. The land was a wooded dairy farm near the Lake Street bridge, accessible by streetcar at the time for "only 5 cents fare from any point in Minneapolis or St. Paul within an area of about one hundred (100) miles in circumference" according to the promotional map. However, the school couldn't hold real estate under the name Minnehaha Academy because it hadn't yet incorporated, so Aaron Carlson, Treasurer of the Board, acquired the title to the land temporarily on December 16, 1904.

On January 11, 1905, seventeen men led by Daniel Magnus met during a blizzard at Bethany Covenant Church in south Minneapolis where they deliberated, prayed, and voted to begin a Christian high school. Because of the snow storm, travel by road was shut down, so some of the members walked through the night back to their homes in St. Paul while others stayed at the church overnight and walked home the next day. Shortly after this meeting, the Minnehaha Academy Association was formed and the school was incorporated on January 18, 1905, under the name of Minnehaha Academy with the purpose "to furnish young men and women with the essential elements of a liberal education, and to foster the development of character under the personal influence of Christian teachers" as stated in Article I of the original Articles of Incorporation. Following its incorporation, Minnehaha Academy purchased the twenty-eight acres of land from Aaron Carlson on April 30, 1906. The money for the purchase was raised by donations from the members of the Minnehaha Academy Association. In 1908, sixteen of the twenty-eight acres were sold, and the money earned from the sale was set aside for a building fund.

(Photo reproduction courtesy of Jim Nash)

Daniel Magnus.

In 1909, the Minnehaha Academy Association offered its assets to the Northwestern Mission Society, an organization of the Swedish Mission churches in the Northwest, with the understanding that the society would take charge of the school and construct a school building within a reasonable amount of time. The offer was accepted in May 1910. However, the land remained empty until 1911 while efforts were being made to raise enough money to pay for the construction of a school.

The Corps of Collectors gathered in a circle on the undeveloped ground of the school during the annual conference of the Northwestern Young People's Covenant, July 30, 1911.

(Photo from the MA archives, reproduction courtesy of Jim Nash)

THE COST OF EDUCATION

Two figures were instrumental in raising money for the new school. Daniel Magnus, who had helped find the land on which to build the school, traveled throughout the Northwest, scheduling lectures and concerts in order to raise interest and money and establish a fundraising organization called the Minnehaha Reserves in 1906.

Andrew L. Skoog was a musician, educator, and close friend of E. A. Skogsbergh. Skoog was also a constant promoter of Minnehaha Academy during and after its establishment. He provided the use of his own home as a fundraising headquarters, published motivational articles, and recognized the school's supporters in issues of the *Veckobladet*. Skoog was also a composer who wrote more than 300 anthems and hymn tunes in his lifetime. In addition to the songs he wrote for the Swedish Mission Covenant, he also wrote original songs intended to inspire people to give to the school.

The Constitution of the Minnehaha Reserves was adopted on February 14, 1906.

A. L. Skoog.

(Image from the MA archives)

(Photo courtesy of First Covenant Church, Minneapolis archives)

Swedish Roots: 1884–1913   11

In July 1911, the annual conference of the Northwestern Young People's Covenant was held on the undeveloped land of the school. At that conference a Corps of Collectors was established and Skoog led the Corps' efforts to raise $25,000 in ten months. To encourage people to give, the Minnehaha Legion was created to recognize those who gave a minimum of twenty-five dollars for the building fund. In return, these donors were awarded with diploma-like certificates. The Corps ended up raising more than $27,000.

Skoog was a leader by example, donating himself while encouraging others to do the same. Skoog's personal record book, marked as No. 1, provides an appeal to the public for Minnehaha Academy as well as endorsements by the Board of the Northwestern Mission

(Photo from the MA archives)

Society in Swedish and English. The book also lists personal endorsements by prominent individuals.

While money was being raised for the new school building, the currently operating school closed in May 1911.

The first bids for construction of the new building began to come in on August 1, 1912. On September 8,

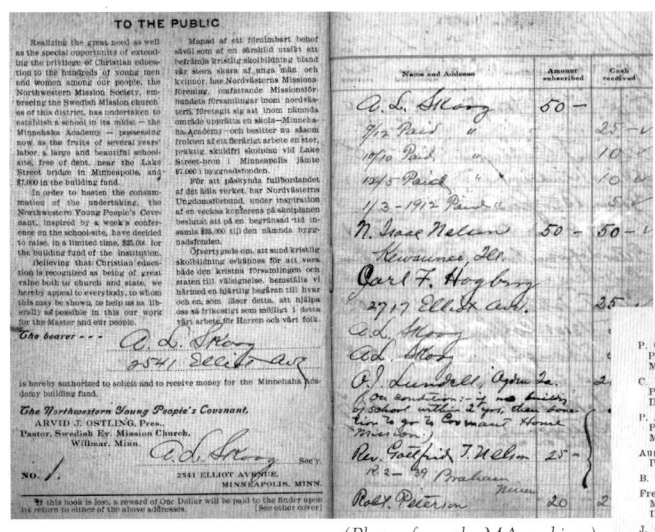

(Photos from the MA archives)

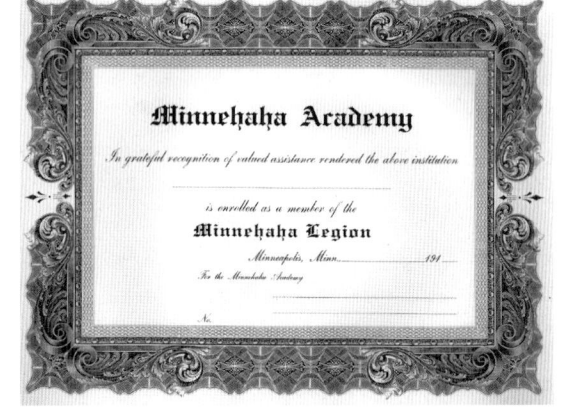

12 MINNEHAHA ACADEMY: A CENTURY OF FAITH AND LEARNING

(Photo from the MA archives)

1912, Reverend E. A. Skogsbergh laid the first cornerstone.

The newly completed building was dedicated on June 21, 1913. In August 1913, Skoog urged the Corps of Collectors to make a final push to gather funds so the newly constructed school building would be properly furnished with items such as blackboards, a piano, chairs, typewriters, a kitchen stove, and electric hall bells (Nordstrom 2001, 43).

On Wednesday, September 3, a rally was held in the chapel to honor the Corps of Collectors for their hard work in gathering contributions from numerous donors. A Roll of Honor listing the names of those who had given one hundred dollars or more from 1911 to 1913 was personally penned by A. L. Skoog, framed, and hung in the school's chapel in 1915. The Roll of Honor still hangs in the North Campus today.

(Photo from the MA archives)

With the building bought and paid for, the brand-new school of Minnehaha Academy opened debt-free.

(Photo from the MA archives)

SWEDISH ROOTS: 1884–1913   13

Minnehaha Academy is intimately tied to its location along the Mississippi River in Minneapolis. The school signs displayed along the River Road are a prominent feature of the school. The signs have changed over the decades as much as the look of the school buildings.

(Image from the MA archives)

The 1953–1954 PTA took on the project of purchasing a brick-and-metal sign for the school at a cost of $500.

Mrs. Margaret Wallentine (class of 1933), her husband Stanley Wallentine, and Gordon Wallentine (class of 1929) provided the school with the memorial gift of a white-and-gold-lettered Colonial sign that was placed on the 47th Avenue side of Minnehaha Academy in the 1960s.

The Colonial sign was displayed at the back of the school and a brick-and-metal sign was displayed along the River Road in the 1960s and 1970s.

(Image from the MA archives)

(Image from the MA archives)

New lighted signs were installed on February 22, 1982, at the North and South campuses. They were purchased from Universal Sign Company at an installation cost of approximately $4,600.

(Photos from the MA archives)

The school has updated its signs over the years as they've needed to be repaired or replaced.

The Academy plans to install new signs for the Centennial celebration. The signs will feature digital displays. Provided is a conceptual rendering of what the signs will look like, but you are welcome to see them for yourself on a drive by or visit to the campuses.

(Photo courtesy of Jim Nash)

(Rendering courtesy of Spectrum Sign Systems, Inc., used by permission)

SWEDISH ROOTS: 1884–1913

1913–1919

(Photos courtesy of Jim Nash)

16 Minnehaha Academy: A Century of Faith and Learning

Minnehaha Academy officially began its first year in its new school building on Monday, September 15, 1913. The hard work of erecting a school building was over, but the hard work of ensuring that the building stayed open and the school proved successful had just begun. The first years of Minnehaha Academy's experience proved to be a time of rapid growth. In just three years, the school launched its first building campaign, the Thousand Tens, raising $10,000 for the building's first addition. Despite concerns about the impact of the First World War on enrollment, the student body also expanded in the first six years. Nine students came to the school when it opened in September 1913, but by the end of the school year, enrollment reached 112. The student body tripled in 1918–1919 to 336. In 1918, over thirty of the school's former students were enlisted in military and naval service and a large service flag with a star for each of the boys was hung in the school's chapel.

Minnehaha Academy printed small pamphlets and catalogs in the early years as advertising material. The Academy did not publish a yearbook or a school newspaper in the 1910s.

Reverend Theodore W. Anderson received the call to become Minnehaha Academy's first president at the age of twenty-four. In a 1968 address to the Minnehaha Fellowship, Anderson recalled what it was like becoming president of a school at such a young age, saying, "I never knew, until I had received and accepted the call to be the first president, that when the matter was considered in the board of directors of the school, there were some who said he's too young and inexperienced. Maybe they were right. But the chairman of the board, Reverend C. F. Sandstrom of the Salem Covenant Church in Minneapolis, defended the recommendation and said that if it's a handicap to be young, it's one from which you gradually grow away. I realize the validity of that, increasingly, as the years slip by." Anderson accepted the call on the condition that he be given a year to complete his work on a master's degree at the University of Chicago. He received his Master of Arts degree in June 1914 and assumed the full responsibilities of the presidency at the start of the 1914 school year.

(Photo from the MA archives)

(Photo courtesy of Covenant Archives and Historical Library, North Park University, Chicago, Illinois)

Reverend Nathaniel Franklin, vice-chairman of the school board, served as acting president for the 1913–1914 school year while T. W. Anderson was completing his master's degree in Chicago. Franklin held the role of acting president while also continuing as pastor of the Elim Covenant Church in Minneapolis. In 1919, Franklin was elected Sunday School secretary for the Covenant denomination and held that position until 1945.

(Photo reproduction courtesy of Jim Nash)

Joseph E. Burns was head of the Music Department and a teacher of piano, pipe organ, harmony, and theory. He composed the music for the school song. Burns passed away on October 18, 1924.

(Photo reproduction courtesy of Jim Nash)

Marie Ackerlund-Omark began giving instruction in violin in the fall of 1917 and soon after organized the school's orchestra.

(Photo reproduction courtesy of Jim Nash)

Reverend Daniel Bloomdahl graduated from Minnehaha Academy in 1917. Bloomdahl wrote the lyrics to the school song. He later became a teaching assistant in the High School Department in 1919 and then a teacher of Swedish and English in 1923. He was involved in the music program and served as athletic director, continuing at the Academy until 1928. He returned to teach history from 1957 until 1959.

(Photo from the MA archives)

Lillian Oberg joined the faculty on August 17, 1917. She worked as an office secretary and bookkeeper and then as secretary to President T. W. Anderson. She also served as secretary for the Alumni Association. Oberg retired in 1958.

(Photo reproduction courtesy of Jim Nash)

Ezra N. Oberg, Lillian Oberg's brother, started at the Academy in 1919. He taught shorthand, business law, business practice, economics, and office training. In 1920, he became the head of the Business Department. Ezra Oberg continued at the school until 1942.

(Photo courtesy of Bethlehem Covenant Church)

Peter J. Edquist was the Academy's first janitor in 1913. He was also the founder of the Minnehaha Academy Sunday School, which later developed into Bethlehem Covenant Church. Edquist died on December 25, 1922.

MINNEHAHA ACADEMY
MINNEAPOLIS, MINN.

First School Year Begins
Monday, September 15
1913

FACULTY.

THEODORE W. ANDERSON, President.
(A. B., University of Chicago).
(On leave of absence 1913-1914).

REV. NATH. FRANKLIN, Acting President.
(A. B., University of Minnesota).
Christianity.

A. LEONARD WEDELL.
(A. M., Northwestern University).
History, Latin, Swedish.

ETHEL R. MATSON.
(A. B., University of Minnesota).
English, Mathematics.

E. G. EKBLAD, Head of Commercial Dept.
(M. Acct., Bethany College, Lindsborg, Kan.)
Bookkeeping, Shorthand, etc.

JOSEPH E. BURNS, Head of Music Dept.
Piano, Pipe Organ, Harmony.

One of the school's earliest pamphlets from 1913 lists just six teachers as faculty.

(Images from the MA archives and courtesy of Jim Nash)

1913–1919 19

1913–1919
IN THE BEGINNING

MINNEHAHA ACADEMY was located thirty-five minutes from the downtowns of Minneapolis and St. Paul in what was then still a largely rural area. Most students in the early years came from outside the cities to attend the Academy. Students from Michigan, North Dakota, South Dakota, Nebraska, Wisconsin, and throughout Minnesota attended the school. Travel was available by streetcar at a rate of five cents from any point in Minneapolis or St. Paul. Board was available at the school for three dollars a week and lodging was available in the neighborhood for as little as three dollars a month. The school office kept records of the families in the neighborhood who opened their houses to take in students. The Academy also operated a bureau of employment at the school to help students secure work in the cities for those who sought to pay their tuition on their own.

WELCOME TO MINNEHAHA ACADEMY!

47th Avenue South and 31st Street
Minneapolis, Minn.

DEPARTMENTS:
ACADEMIC: High School
PREPARATORY: Swedish-English
COMMERCIAL: All business subjects
MUSIC: Piano, Violin, Voice
SUMMER SCHOOL
EVENING SCHOOL

ADVANTAGES:
New well equipped building   Twelve acres of beautiful campus
One fare from any point in Twin Cities   Thorough instruction and reasonable rates
Christian influences

Summer School is held in the Music and Commercial Departments. Complete courses in Bookkeeping, Shorthand, Typewriting, Commercial Law, etc.
Term of 10 weeks begins next Tuesday, June 1. Tuition for term is $17.50
For further particulars write the school or telephone T. S. Snelling 128.

(Image from the MA archives)

This 1915 advertisement for the school was printed on the back of one of the school's music programs.

Tuition per eighteen-week term ranged from eighteen dollars in the Academic Department to thirty dollars in the Commercial Department. The Academy also operated an Evening School offering courses from the Commercial Department and a Summer School offering commercial and music courses. Minnehaha Academy's Christian emphasis was a prominent part of the school from the very beginning. Attendance at chapel services and in Bible courses was required of every student. It was also expected that all students would attend worship on Sundays, at the church of their or their parents' choosing.

Boys and girls ate at separate tables in the dining hall in the early decades of the school.

(Photo from the MA archives)

20 MINNEHAHA ACADEMY: A CENTURY OF FAITH AND LEARNING

Classes at the Academy were held on Tuesdays through Saturdays. The reason for this practice was that students and faculty often participated in morning and evening services on Sundays at churches in rural areas, so Mondays were reserved for travel back to the city on back roads and remote highways (Nordstrom 2001, 185–186). Classes began at 9 a.m. Each period was forty-five minutes long. After two periods, the school gathered for chapel. Chapel was followed by two more periods, then classes were dismissed for a noon recess. Three periods were held in the afternoon and school ended at 3:30 p.m. One of the earliest annual school events was Campus Day, when all the teachers and students spent the day with rakes, shovels, and other equipment, cleaning up the campus grounds.

Minnehaha Academy opened with four main departments: Academic, Preparatory, Commercial, and Music.

The Academic Department was the high school, offering three prescribed courses: the Classical, the Modern Language, and the Scientific.

The Preparatory Department provided coursework equivalent to seventh and eighth grades in public schools for students lacking the education necessary to enter the high school and for students who did not receive their education in America and needed training in English.

The Commercial Department provided training for business, including bookkeeping, shorthand, typewriting, and civil service courses. Civil service courses prepared students to take civil service examinations for positions such as stenographer, typist, mail carrier, post office clerk, or railway mail clerk.

The Music Department offered voice and theory courses as well as instrumental instruction in piano, organ, and violin. Music played a prominent role in the school both academically and as an extracurricular activity. Joseph E. Burns organized and conducted the Minnehaha Choral Society in 1915.

The Minnehaha Choral Society was an oratorio chorus numbering over 200 members drawn from Minnehaha Academy and the Swedish Mission Churches of the Twin Cities. During Commencement Week in 1915, the chorus gave two renditions of Haydn's *The Creation*, one in St. Paul and the other in Minneapolis.

Marie Ackerlund-Omark, pictured with her students in 1918, formed the first school orchestra.

(Photo from the MA archives)

EVERYTHING A FIRST

- In the spring of 1914, the first class graduated fourteen students from Minnehaha Academy, soon after inspiring the formation of an Alumni Association, which quickly grew, as the number of graduates in 1918 exceeded seventy-five.

- The class of 1915, the first to present a memorial gift to the school, donated a drinking fountain.

- The faculty made the motion to choose the school's colors as crimson and white in 1914.

- The faculty organized the school's first Student Council in 1918. Representatives were elected from each of the departments and the council was given general charge over the interests of the student body.

- The very first student activities to be organized were a Prayer Band, which met at six o'clock on Monday evenings for prayer, and a Literary Society that hosted speeches, essays, debates, and music by students, members of the faculty, and occasionally outside guests.

- Minnehaha Academy received accreditation from the University of Minnesota before the first high school class graduated. Accreditation meant that graduates could attend the U of M without needing to take an exam.

AROUND CAMPUS

The school advertised its location along the banks of the Mississippi River as ideally suited for such activities as cross-country running, boating, and skating. An athletic field for baseball was prepared, a tennis court was available, and basketball equipment was set up. Courses in calisthenics were provided outdoors and indoors during the winters. A Minnehaha Athletic Association was created to arrange all interscholastic events. Shower baths could be used all season and steel lockers were installed and available for rent by the students. The school's athletic field could not be used during school hours, and during the day students who were at school but not in class were required to be in the study room.

(Photo from the MA archives)

The preservation of Swedish heritage marked early concerns for the school community. In a publication titled *Minnehaha Call* (August 1912), Erik Dahlhielm, editor of the Swedish-language newspaper *Veckobladet*, provided three reasons for Minnehaha Academy, which included the following: "We need the school for the sake of the Mission Covenant work. The Swedish Mission Covenant's future depends from a human point of view on the education we seek to give young people. If they come entirely under the influence of American schools, we cannot expect but that the interest for the Swedish work shall be lost" (P. Anderson 1984, 80). All students of Swedish descent were required to take two years of Swedish in order to graduate. According to the 1913–1914 Catalog, "The promoters of Minnehaha Academy are men and women, who highly prize Swedish art and culture, and who believe that by fostering the language of their native country in the land of their adoption, they may perpetuate the literary treasures bequeathed to them by their fathers. For this reason, a strong emphasis is placed on the study of the Swedish language."

(Image from the MA archives)

22 MINNEHAHA ACADEMY: A CENTURY OF FAITH AND LEARNING

IF THESE FLOORBOARDS
COULD SPEAK...

Daniel Bloomdahl '17 related his experience of writing the school song several decades after he graduated:

"...The idea was to furnish a school yell that could be used at basketball games... A committee of three was appointed to prepare and submit some school yells or chorus. I tried individually to do something of the kind, and in the progress, the proposed school yell came to be, much to my surprise, the official school song.

"I don't recall the details of writing it. I think the opening lines popped into my mind as I was walking to school one morning during my senior year. It developed over a period of several days, and when it was finally committed to paper, chorus and all, I knew that it was anything but a yell.

"I submitted the draft to President T. W. Anderson, who showed it to Mr. A. L. Skoog. They presented it to the School Board recommending that it be adopted as the school song. Joseph Burns, head of the Music Department, composed the melody. [...]

"There have been changes at the Academy since the writing of the School Song. None of the same teachers remain on the staff. New buildings have been added, and the old one altered from time to time. The number of courses offered and the extra curricular and interschool activities available is much greater. There is a larger student body. But with all these changes we are grateful that the fine Christian spirit and atmosphere of the Academy remain the same."

(Quiver, April 22, 1953)

(Images from the MA archives)

MA's school song was submitted to the U.S. Copyright Office and officially published on April 25, 1917.

A CHRISTIAN SCHOOL

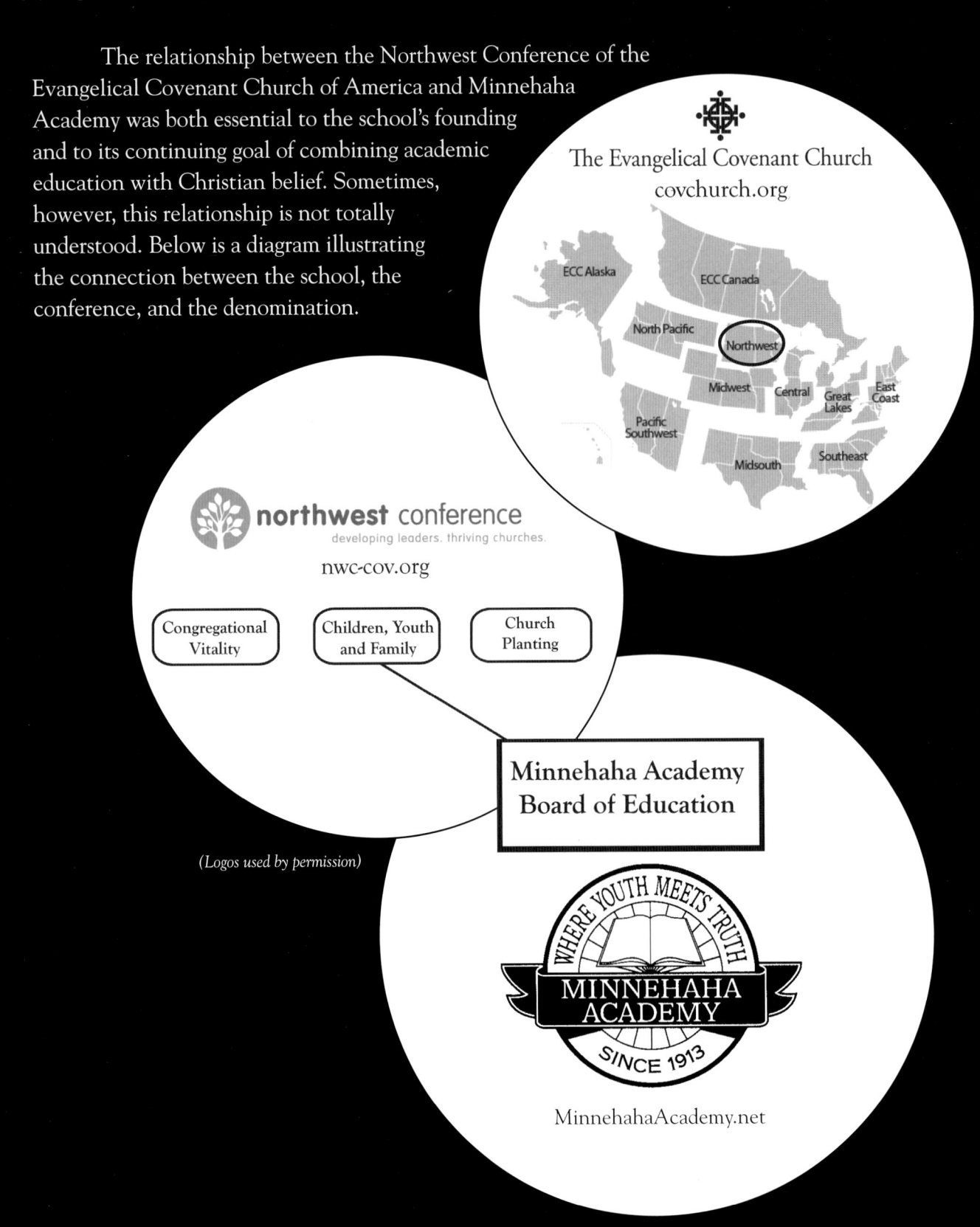

The relationship between the Northwest Conference of the Evangelical Covenant Church of America and Minnehaha Academy was both essential to the school's founding and to its continuing goal of combining academic education with Christian belief. Sometimes, however, this relationship is not totally understood. Below is a diagram illustrating the connection between the school, the conference, and the denomination.

The Evangelical Covenant Church
covchurch.org

northwest conference
developing leaders. thriving churches.
nwc-cov.org

Congregational Vitality | Children, Youth and Family | Church Planting

Minnehaha Academy Board of Education

WHERE YOUTH MEETS TRUTH
MINNEHAHA ACADEMY
SINCE 1913

MinnehahaAcademy.net

(Logos used by permission)

24　Minnehaha Academy: A Century of Faith and Learning

The Evangelical Covenant Church (ECC) is a Christian Protestant denomination composed of over 800 congregations in the United States and Canada and ministries on five continents. The ECC was established in 1885 as the Swedish Evangelical Mission Covenant of America. The Northwest Conference (NWC) was established in 1884 as the Swedish Christian Mission Association of the Northwest. A year after its founding it became a regional branch of the larger Covenant denomination. The NWC is made up of more than 140 churches in Minnesota, North and South Dakota, Iowa, and western Wisconsin.

The NWC owns Minnehaha Academy as an important extension of its commitment to children, youth, and family ministry, and its vision to develop leaders for thriving churches. Pastors of Covenant churches and the superintendent of the Northwest Conference sit on the school's Board of Education. The Board is accountable to the Conference when undertaking major building or fundraising campaigns, while the Academy's day-to-day operation remains the responsibility of the school's administration, faculty, and staff.

(Photo from the MA archives)

For many years the Northwest Conference office was located in the former president's house on 47th Avenue in Minneapolis. In late 1978, a new building was constructed at the North Campus, which stood until it was taken down in 2001 in preparation for construction of the new gymnasium. After the former president's house was remodeled, the Northwest Conference once again moved back into that space.

In addition to extending the ministry of the Conference and the Covenant, Minnehaha has also been a source of strength for both. Throughout its history, students from Covenant families across the United States have come to Minneapolis to attend MA. The school has been a place where generations of Conference and Covenant pastors, missionaries, and lay leaders have learned, taught, and experienced God's call in their lives. The Academy has also hosted both Conference and denominational annual meetings. For many people, Minnehaha Academy has been and continues to be one of the most visible expressions of the Covenant's ministry in the Northwest.

The former president's house at 3106 47th Avenue S was originally built for T. W. Anderson. The house now provides space for the offices of the Northwest Conference.

(Photo from the MA archives)

1920–1929

(Photos courtesy of Jim Nash)

26 Minnehaha Academy: A Century of Faith and Learning

MINNEHAHA ACADEMY continued to rapidly expand in the 1920s. Enrollment reached its highest levels since the school's opening, 485 students in 1921–1922—more than four times the number of students in 1913. The Academy launched its third building campaign in 1921, adding a separate auditorium building next to the original building. The first issue of the *Quiver*, the school's student newspaper, was released in October 1920. The school also opened a Bible Institute as a new department in October 1921. Enrollment at the Academy began to decrease toward the end of the decade and the school wouldn't exceed its current record number of students until 1950.

The first *Antler* yearbook was published in 1921 and dedicated to the school president, Theodore Wilbur Anderson. The *Antlers* were not yet produced annually. During the 1920s, they were published every other year. The 1923 *Antler* was dedicated to A. L. Skoog. The 1925 *Antler* was dedicated to Joseph E. Burns, head of the Music Department since the school's opening. Burns passed away on October 18, 1924. The 1927 *Antler* was dedicated to Professor Daniel Magnus. The 1929 *Antler* was dedicated to Rev. E. August Skogsbergh.

Frank Justus Hollinbeck was a teacher at Minnehaha Academy from 1920 to 1946. Hollinbeck graduated from North Park Academy, Chicago, in 1902. Two years later he became one of the first graduates of North Park Junior College. He went on to earn his A.B. degree from the University of Chicago in 1908. In 1920, he left Chicago and moved to Minneapolis, where he joined the faculty of Minnehaha. He served in various capacities at the school, including as teacher of history, English, German, and Bible, head of the High School Department, principal, librarian, and Philatelic (stamp-collecting) Society advisor. Hollinbeck retired in 1946.

(Photo reproduction courtesy of Jim Nash)

(Photo reproduction courtesy of Jim Nash)

Anna Fellroth came to Minnehaha Academy in 1925. Fellroth taught math and was the girls' athletic director until 1937. She also served as associate principal and principal. She retired in 1963. Her tenure spanned the administrations of all the presidents of the school up to that time, from T. W. Anderson to Wilbur Westerdahl.

(Photo reproduction courtesy of Jim Nash)

Henry Schoultz taught science and served as the school registrar from 1921 to 1943.

Gertrude Sandberg taught Swedish and Latin and served as the girls' advisor at Minnehaha Academy from 1920 to 1952.

(Photo reproduction courtesy of Jim Nash)

(Photo from the MA archives)

John Strandberg was a Swedish immigrant who came to the U.S. when he was twenty-two. He received a few months of preparatory schooling at Minnehaha Academy in 1916 in his application for citizenship papers. He became janitor of the school in 1928, after a drought hit his farm in North Dakota. He was paid sixty-seven dollars a month, and his family lived in a rent-free house on campus (the original farmhouse of the property). Strandberg's wife Anna worked as a cook in the school kitchen (Nordstrom 2001, 187–188). In 1935, Strandberg left the school to become custodian at First Covenant Church, Minneapolis. He returned to Minnehaha Academy in 1946 and served in his role until 1960. During that time, his three sons all became graduates of the school (*Covenant Weekly*, February 12, 1954).

Sella V. Nelson, or Sella V. as she was known by many, taught typewriting, business English, and shorthand for thirty-two years. She retired in 1952.

(Photo reproduction courtesy of Jim Nash)

28 MINNEHAHA ACADEMY: A CENTURY OF FAITH AND LEARNING

ROARING MINNEHAHA

Minnehaha Academy dropped its Preparatory Department as a division of the school in the 1920s, but a high school preparatory course was still offered as part of the High School Department. Night School was also discontinued. Despite these shifts, the school provided a special short course in any subject for students who were needed to work at home and could only attend school for a few months at a time. The short course did not grant a diploma, but a record was kept of the subjects finished so that students could eventually earn a diploma after meeting the sufficient number of credits.

Students held prayer meetings every morning at 8:45 a.m. and every Tuesday evening. Students also held Thursday noonday meetings of singing and sharing testimonies. In addition to services on campus, students led services at the Scandinavian Union Mission, the Volunteers of America, and the Rescue Mission.

The school established a laundry agency for use by students because many students who attended the Academy still came from outside the cities. The school's janitor managed the laundry agency. For those living out of town, the bookstore provided a case for mailing laundry back home.

Chewing gum was prohibited and only non-spillable inkwells were allowed in the school. Playing ball or throwing snowballs was not permitted on the campuses between 47th and 48th Avenues. Students also weren't allowed to drive automobiles to classes except by special permission. This rule did not apply to faculty and staff, however. The Board of Directors, faculty, and friends of President Anderson presented him with a new Dodge Sedan on Tuesday, November 23, 1920, in appreciation of his work and as a token of gratitude for rejecting an offer to become president of North Park College and instead remain as president of Minnehaha Academy. The next day Anderson drove his new car to school.

BIBLE INSTITUTE OPENS

The Academy opened a Bible Institute as a new department in October 1921. The Bible Institute was primarily designed for training lay workers in the church. The faculty consisted of Swedish Mission ministers and members of the faculty from other departments at Minnehaha Academy. Erik Dahlhielm, editor of *Veckobladet*, even taught courses in Early and Modern Church History. Professor T. W. Anderson, Reverend Herbert Palmquist, and Reverend A. Milton Freedholm headed the institute at different times in the 1920s. Classes were taught in English and Swedish because knowledge of both was essential in churches that still spoke primarily Swedish. Tuition was free for the first years of the institute's operation, but later cost fifteen dollars per semester. All students were expected to have actual experience in doing Christian work while at the institute.

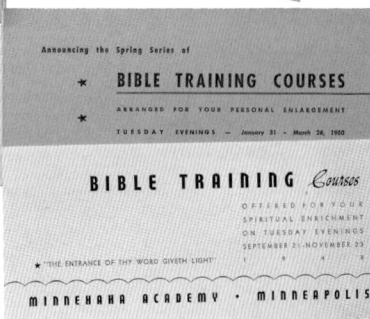

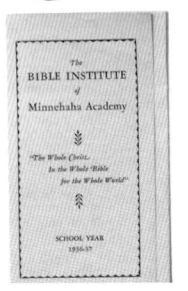

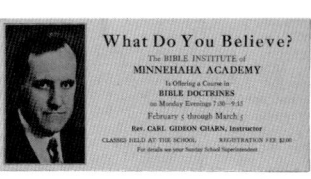

(Photos courtesy of Jim Nash)

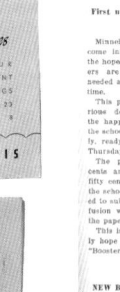

QUIVER LAUNCHED
(ARROW TO FOLLOW AFTER)

The first issue of the *Quiver*, the school's student newspaper, was released in October 1920, and published with a giant question mark at the top of it in place of a title. Students and teachers were encouraged to submit suggestions for names for the newspaper. The name *Quiver* was suggested by A. L. Skoog and accepted by the newspaper's editor. According to the paper, "In Longfellow's poem, Hiawatha travels to an ancient Arrow-maker at Minnehaha. Associated with arrows is the quiver, a receptacle used by the Indians to keep their arrows in. Our paper will be a 'Quiver' in that it will hold the 'arrows' of school life. Not those which will kill and destroy but those which will help and brighten our school days" (*Quiver*, Vol. I, No. 2). The *Quiver* was originally made available to students by subscription.

30 MINNEHAHA ACADEMY: A CENTURY OF FAITH AND LEARNING

BURSTING AT THE SEAMS

The much-needed new auditorium addition to the school allowed for the expansion of the school's athletics facilities. A Student Athletic Board was established in the fall of 1923 to govern all athletic affairs in the school. This board was composed of one girl and one boy representative from each class in the High School Department and one girl and one boy representative from the Bible Institute and the Business Department. The board consisted of officers and a Boys' Committee, a Girls' Committee, an Arrangement Committee, and an Equipment Committee.

In an edition of the *Helping Hands Quarterly*, published by the Helping Hands Society, one student provided a graphic representation of how it felt to attend such a crammed school before the construction of the auditorium addition.

Boys' and girls' basketball teams were organized and basketball became one of the school's most prominent sports. The new gymnasium provided a full-size regulation basketball court with locker rooms and shower baths. Prior to the addition, gym space had to be rented off-campus. Interscholastic games were restricted to Christian schools.

GREAT NEED OF A NEW BUILDING,
As Seen By A Student
(Image from the MA archives)

(Photo from the MA archives)

The 1923 girls' basketball team went undefeated during their season.

The Academy played in the Twin City Academic League, consisting of four schools: Augsburg Academy, Bethel Academy, Minnesota College, and Minnehaha Academy. Concordia College was added to the league in 1929. Track and baseball teams were also organized. The track team competed against Bethel Academy and the baseball team competed against several other schools. The girls organized a softball team in 1926, then referred to as "kitten ball."

A FEW FIRSTS OF THE 1920s

- In 1922, the school opened its bookstore. Prior to 1922 books and stationary were purchased in the school office.

- The school held its first Homecoming in 1924 for the class of 1923.

- An Honor Roll was created in 1923.

- The 1963 *Antler* that recorded events in celebration of the school's fifty-year anniversary mentioned that a barber shop was installed in Minnehaha Academy in 1927. A note from "My School Diary" in the 1928 *Quill* records that on Wednesday, October 5, a student "had a hair cut at the new barber shop installed at school, by Bob Sturdy."

- The Minnehaha chapter of the National Forensic League was also established in 1927, making it one of the oldest in the Twin Cities. Among its charter members was E. O. Franklin, the first sponsor of the chapter who would later become president of Minnehaha Academy.

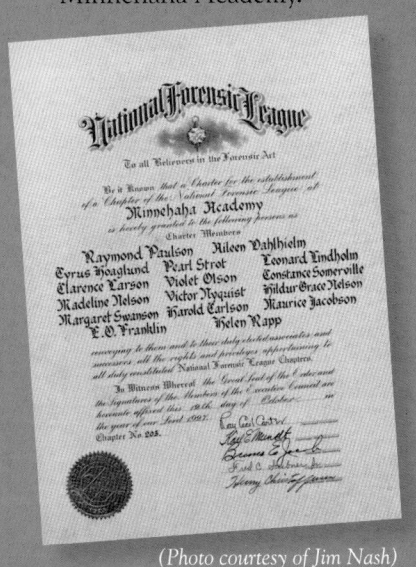

(Photo courtesy of Jim Nash)

AROUND CAMPUS

Speech and debate were prominent activities at the Academy in its earliest years. The Teachers' Committee of the Board of Directors decided to challenge North Park College in Chicago to a debate with the Academy, which was accepted in 1918. This led to the first debate competition against North Park, held in the spring of 1920 in Chicago. The question debated was "Resolved: That the United States should own and operate all railroads doing an interstate business." North Park won, taking the affirmative position. The Academy's debates with North Park then became an annual tradition. The competitions alternated between being hosted in Minneapolis and Chicago. North Park hosted the competition in even years, and MA hosted in odd years. A silver loving cup was later introduced as an award to the school that won in a series of debates over a set number of years. This annual tradition continued until 1944.

Many new student clubs continued to be formed. The school administration experimented with an early point system that would regulate how many offices students could hold in clubs, in order to prevent them from becoming too involved in activities at the cost of their coursework. A Florence Nightingale Society was created for students interested in the nursing profession. The club studied the life of Florence Nightingale, provided demonstrations in the bandaging and dressing of wounds, and visited the Swedish Hospital and Nurses' Dormitory. Funds were raised by means of a handkerchief sale for the purchase of an Emergency Kit, which was presented to the school. The club also took on the responsibility of keeping the kit supplied.

(Image from the MA archvies)

FLORENCE NIGHTINGALE SOCIETY

ALIDA JACOBSON	President
HELEN WILLIAMS	Vice President
SYLVIA PETERSON	Secretary
EVELYNE PETERSON	Treasurer
MARGARET HEGG	Chaplain

(Photo from the MA archives)

IF THESE FLOORBOARDS
COULD SPEAK...

STUDENTS FROM THE GRADUATING CLASS of 1921 petitioned to have their Baccalaureate speech in English instead of Swedish. The Committee on Administration respectfully turned down the petition for a number of reasons:

    a. This is the only event during graduation not conducted in the English language;
    b. The Baccalaureate exercise is held in place of regular Sunday morning service;
    c. Attendance by members of the graduating class is not obligatory;
    d. The Swedish people have built this school and constitute the greater part of the audience on this occasion.
(Nordstrom 2001, 29)

The issue of speaking English or Swedish partly arose from sentiments associated with World War I, as President T. W. Anderson remarked in his recollections of the school's early years:

"In the wake of [World War I], I had a unique class meeting informally every Monday afternoon. In the war hysteria great pressure was brought to bear on all pastors and churches to use the English language exclusively in public services. A bill was actually introduced in the Minnesota legislature to prohibit homes from having any book or periodical in any language but English. Fortunately, it was overwhelmingly defeated. In this emergency some Covenant pastors and a few from other churches asked me to meet with them once a week for practice in preaching in English. Even the pastors of our largest churches in the Twin Cities joined this class and participated in it actively." (T. Anderson 1964, 9)

The original petition from the class of 1921 states, "We the undersigned do hereby petition to have the Baccalaureate sermon delivered in the English Language."

(Images from the MA archives)

Minnehaha Academy has had many different logos representing the school and its many associated programs. Here are just a few of the Academy's marks through the years.

A. L. Skoog promoted the school during campaigns by distributing buttons with the school's logo. In a letter written by Skoog, he remarks that "a waggish friend read it, 'Money Always'—not a bad idea. Perhaps it may also infuse 'More Ambition' and 'Mer Allvar' [more earnestness] into our work" (Nordstrom 2001, 210).

(Photo courtesy of Jim Nash)

The image of Minnehaha Falls reflects the school's connection to its location along the River Road in Minneapolis, Minnesota.

Minnehaha Academy celebrated its fiftieth anniversary in 1963. A few years after the anniversary, the lower half of the logo was removed and the top was used as a general school logo.

The school's mascot was the Indian for over seventy-five years. After a long process of community deliberation, the mascot was changed to the Redhawk in 1990.

Minnehaha Academy celebrated its seventy-fifth anniversary in 1983.

Minnehaha Academy's current school logo retains the school's long-held motto, "Where Youth Meets Truth." After the Centennial celebration, the school will unveil a new logo.

The Centennial logo honors the school's one-hundred-year history from 1913 to 2013.

1920–1929 35

1930–1939

(Photos courtesy of Jim Nash)

36　Minnehaha Academy: A Century of Faith and Learning

Minnehaha Academy was not immune to the effects of the Great Depression in the 1930s. In 1937, the annual conference of the Covenant Church was held at Minnehaha Academy and the school's acting president, Joel S. Peterson, reported that Minnehaha Academy was the only Christian high school of five in the Twin Cities that survived the Depression (*Covenant Weekly*, Friday, May 22, 1953). While other Christian schools closed due to the economic conditions of the times, the Academy managed to stay open because of the support and sacrifice of its community. Enrollment dropped in 1933–1934 to 134 students, the school's lowest point since it opened—barely more than the number of students who attended in 1913–1914. Enrollment began to increase slowly in the second half of the decade. In 1939, the board approved the merging of the Business Department with the High School Department. The school faculty made the decision in 1938 to publish the *Antler* as an annual, and an *Antler* has been released every year since 1939. The 1939 *Antler* commemorated Minnehaha Academy's twenty-fifth anniversary.

The Quill Club was organized as a school literary society in the 1920s. The society produced a publication called the *Quill*, which contained collections of poems, essays, and material from the graduating class as a self-described "sort of souvenir about the graduates." The *Quill* was available by subscription. In the 1930s, the *Quill* was released in alternate even-numbered years to supplement those years when the *Antler* wasn't published.

(Photo from the MA archives)

Mr. Joel S. Peterson, a member of the faculty at Minnehaha Academy, assumed leadership as acting president following T. W. Anderson's departure in 1933. After Reverend Emanuel O. Franklin took up the official position in 1938, Peterson returned to the classroom to teach English until 1941. After his time at Minnehaha, Peterson was ordained a Covenant minister. He returned to Canada, where he was born, and served for ten years as president of the Covenant Bible College. He returned to the U.S. in 1951 and served in several pastorates prior to his retirement in 1963.

Reverend Emanuel O. Franklin, younger brother of Nathaniel Franklin, held a part-time position at Minnehaha Academy as an assistant in the Preparatory Department from 1914 to 1917 while he was a student at Macalester College. Franklin taught science, math, English, and French and was the director of the debate program as a member of the school faculty from 1919 to 1930. He left Minnehaha Academy to become editor of the *Veckobladet* newspaper and then served as the pastor of Salem Covenant Church in Duluth from 1931 to 1938, but returned to become the school's second president.

(Photo reproduction courtesy of Jim Nash)

(Photo from the MA archives)

Lillian Sandberg was an instructor of piano on the music staff from 1939 to 1952.

Professor Robert N. Pearson was the head of Minnehaha Academy's Music Department from 1931 to 1948. He founded the Minnehaha Singers in 1934 and reformed the school's orchestra in 1939. He died suddenly on January 13, 1949.

(Photo from the MA archives)

(Photo from the MA archives)

Joseph R. Adell, former superintendent of schools in McPherson, Kansas, became the first principal of the school in 1938. In addition to this role, he also taught history and Bible and was director of athletics. Adell served at the school until 1943.

38 MINNEHAHA ACADEMY: A CENTURY OF FAITH AND LEARNING

HARD TIMES

Financial struggles throughout the 1930s affected many facets of school life. To conserve fuel, all classes were held in the main building. Instrumental music was largely discontinued during the 1930s due to the decrease in enrollment. Summer School was also discontinued. In 1933, the school grounds and building were mortgaged to pay past-due salary checks and bills and consolidate smaller loans. Members of the faculty and staff were asked to give between 5 percent and 10 percent of their salaries back to the school from 1932 through the school year of 1933–1934. The average amount they gave was 7.2 percent. In 1934, the salaries of everyone on the payroll were reduced by 25 percent, even while some of the school's teachers took on additional responsibilities due to reductions in staff. The faculty numbered nine teachers in 1935.

One way that members of the school sought to save money during the 1930s was to sell off unused school equipment, such as typewriters, due to decreased enrollment in typewriting classes.

The *Quiver* was reduced to a two-page mimeographed sheet in 1932. Mimeographing provided a cheaper method of printing. The paper continued to be mimeographed until the fall of 1936 when, through the efforts of the *Quiver* staff, a larger printed paper was once more published. An editorial in the October 11, 1932 issue described the situation from the perspective of the paper: "'You did not expect to see me in this dress, did you? Well, all I can say is that I'm still alive, I feel quite well again, and hopeful too, though for a while I did not know whether I would be able to survive or not. The fact is I'm broke; but I'm not going to give up; and that is why I have to wear these depression clothes. However, if you like me this way, inspite of my changed appearance, I'm going to call on you twice a month, and all I ask of you is a nickel. You'll bid me welcome, I am sure, as an old friend, and I'll try my best to do you good.' If the *Quiver* could speak, that would be her message. It has become increasingly more difficult to finance our school publication during these days of depression. The staff has therefore decided to discontinue the form in which the paper has been put out heretofore, and issue it in mimeograph form. It was the feeling of the staff that it would be unwise to discontinue the *Quiver* alltogether."

(Photo from the MA archives)

IN THE ABSENCE OF ANDERSON

The 1930s ushered in more than just financial changes to the school's operation. In the fall of 1932, T. W. Anderson submitted a letter of resignation to the school board in order to serve as president of the Covenant denomination. The board initially rejected his resignation, so Anderson proposed that he be granted a two-year leave of absence to serve as president of the Covenant during the unexpired term of current Covenant president Reverend C. V. Bowman and that a member of the present teaching staff be selected to serve as the Academy's acting president. His request was accepted and his leave without pay went into effect at the end of the school year in 1933, though the board still allowed him to occupy the president's home on the campus during that time. Joel S. Peterson assumed leadership as acting president in Anderson's absence. Anderson's move, however, became permanent when Bowman retired in 1933 due to ill health. Peterson continued to serve in his new role until Reverend Emanuel O. Franklin was selected as the second president of the school in 1938.

At the same time, the board deemed it necessary for the school to have both a president representing the school in the field and a principal to care for administrative work on campus. In the fall of 1938, Joseph R. Adell became the school's principal. The board had also created another new position of field secretary in 1935. The sole function of the field secretary was to raise funds and secure students for the school.

Students studied in the science labs of the 1930s.

(Photos from the MA archives)

40   MINNEHAHA ACADEMY: A CENTURY OF FAITH AND LEARNING

UNDAUNTED ON THE FIELD

Student athletics continued to grow. Girls competed internally in games such as basketball, volleyball, and softball, but did not hold regular games with teams from other schools. The annual classic in girls' basketball was the game between the juniors and seniors. Girls from the Business and Bible Institute departments also fielded an intramural team. The girls received letters for attending gym classes regularly and participating in the basketball tournament. Golf began to develop as a sport at the school starting with a trial year in 1935. Tennis also started to develop. Cheerleaders and a pep band were organized to rouse support at athletic events. The school held its first Winter Sports Day on January 4, 1935. Activities included tobogganing, snowshoeing, and skiing. The school's athletic director, Gordon Granberg, even invited Ambrose Lund, 1933 Canadian ski-jumping champion, to demonstrate stunts.

These early images of six-man football at the Academy were captured off sixteen-millimeter film from 1939.

(Digitization of the film courtesy of Saving Tape and Thor Anderson)

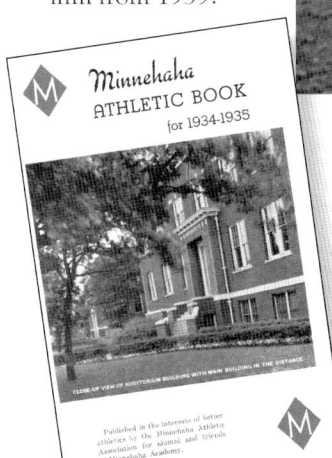

In 1938, students made a request to the board to consider six-man football as a major sport at the school. After deliberation, the board accepted with the provision that the players be insured or the school be absolved from liability for injuries and medical expenses. The six-man format was designed for smaller schools that desired the popular fall sport but would have a hard time maintaining an eleven-man team. The rules of six-man football were modified slightly to account for the smaller teams and to promote safe gameplay.

YEARS OF JUBILEE

In 1937, a Silver Jubilee Campaign was launched to raise $50,000 that would wipe out the school's prevailing indebtedness. The campaign ended on a Victory Sunday on March 20, 1938. The campaign followed the Covenant denomination's Golden Jubilee Year in 1934–1935 when the Covenant established a Jubilee Fund goal of $100,000 to wipe out its debt.

(Images from the MA archives)

A FEW FIRSTS OF THE 1930s

- The school graduated its first two second-generation students, Lorraine Swenson and Gerald Gustafson, in 1938. Gerald Gustafson's father and mother both graduated from Minnehaha Academy. His father, Reverend Henry A. Gustafson, class of 1916, was the first student to register at the Academy. His mother, Esther Peterson Gustafson, graduated in 1918.

- Roland Nelson, class of 1933, formed the "M" Club in 1935. The club was open to all Academy students and alumni who lettered in sports. Members of the club received passes and were granted a special section at athletic events.

- The graduating class of 1937 started a fund for a motion picture projector, which was purchased by the graduating class of 1938. Films were rented from the Visual Education Department of the University of Minnesota, benefiting the student body, individual classes, and the Camera Club.

- Muriel Johnson, class of 1932, was identified as Minnehaha's first cheerleader in the November 1969 *Arrow*.

AROUND CAMPUS

On March 27, 1934, the Minnehaha Singers, led by Robert Pearson, made their debut over station WDGY. They sang four numbers. Marjorie Hognander accompanied at the piano and her brother, Orville Hognander, announced the selections. The Singers took their first out-of-town trip in 1936, traveling to Duluth, Minnesota.

Student clubs continued to develop. A Minnehaha Gospel Team was formed with the sole aim to spread the Gospel. The team conducted services on Sundays and visited homes, distributing Christian literature and giving personal testimonies.

The Council of Christian Activities was formed to encourage more students to participate in Christian activities, particularly giving programs at various churches around the Twin Cities.

(Photos from the MA archives)

42 MINNEHAHA ACADEMY: A CENTURY OF FAITH AND LEARNING

If These Floorboards
could speak...

"CAMPUS DAY"
BY DAVID CURRER '37

"CAN YOU HANDLE a rake, shovel, wheelbarrow, or bushel basket? If you can we want you to help clean up our school campus." With such inspired words the student council enticed the students whom they represent to give up classes for an afternoon and try the other aspects of loafing.

Theoretically campus day is the day when all students help to clean the campus, thus making our school beautiful to say the least. Practically—well—let's speak of what really did happen: In the morning all the bright and sunny cherubes brought their tools, old clothes, and playthings to school with them. When the Chapel period arrived Cecil Osterberg read the rules and regulations. All students heard them in a sort of passive manner. By afternoon they must have forgotten that there ever was such a document proclaimed unto them. One could not say that they did not behave but they were merely a trifle mischievous. Of course the work was done. Through the kind persuation [sic] of Mr. Shoultz, the lazy seniors lifted their weary frames from the grass under the trees and tried to look industrious. The juniors (who have not yet arrived at that totally useless state) did some work even when they were not watched. For an average workman the sophomores were pretty good but for real industry, feats of strength, examples of persistence, and results the freshmen beat the whole school. In fact, a freshman can do the work of two sophomores, three juniors, and at least five seniors. (Figures used by permission of Mr. Shoultz, eminent authority on senior ambition.)

When the campus looked somewhat respectable once more, everyone was fed "gratis". Then came the games, and the walks by the river for those few folks who were interested. Incidently [sic], Miss Mitlyng and Miss Johnson are good enough kittenball players for any girls' team. Miss Mitlyng swings like a rusty gate and Miss Johnson's specialty is chasing fouls (baseball variety).

(*Quiver*, May 5, 1937)

(Photo from the MA archives)

Campus Day was a regular tradition started in the first decade of the school. A few pages from the personal scrapbook of Alice E. C. Landquist depict students and faculty side-by-side, hard at work.

Minnehaha Academy is supported by a broad community, which includes churches of the Northwest Conference, parent volunteers, alumni, and individual donors. The school owes its success as much to the fundraising efforts of this community as to its founders.

A. L. Skoog organized the Helping Hands Society in 1914 to take up the work of collecting money for the school's operating budget. The number five, corresponding to the five fingers of an open hand featured in the Society's logo, was an important part of the Society's structure. The Board of Directors was made up of five members. Membership in the Society was based on a contribution of five dollars annually over a period of five years, and each member was to recruit at least five new members.

(Image from the MA archives)

Covenant women have also significantly contributed to the school's continued success. In the 1930s, the school's Board of Directors asked the Twin Cities branches of the Covenant Women's Auxiliary to help alleviate the school's debt by organizing fundraising concerts for the school. The auxiliary even made gowns for the Minnehaha Academy Singers. The Covenant Women's Auxiliary Benefit Concert became an annual tradition that continued for several decades.

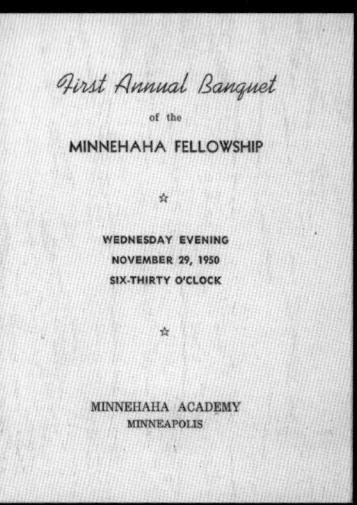

In 1949, Reverend Clarence Nelson, C. Milton Carlson of Bethlehem Covenant Church, and Elmer Johnson and Curtis Johnson of Salem Covenant Church formed the Minnehaha Fellowship. Each member of the Fellowship pledged a minimum annual contribution of fifty dollars toward the current operational needs of the school. To honor its members, the Fellowship hosted its first annual dinner on November 29, 1950.

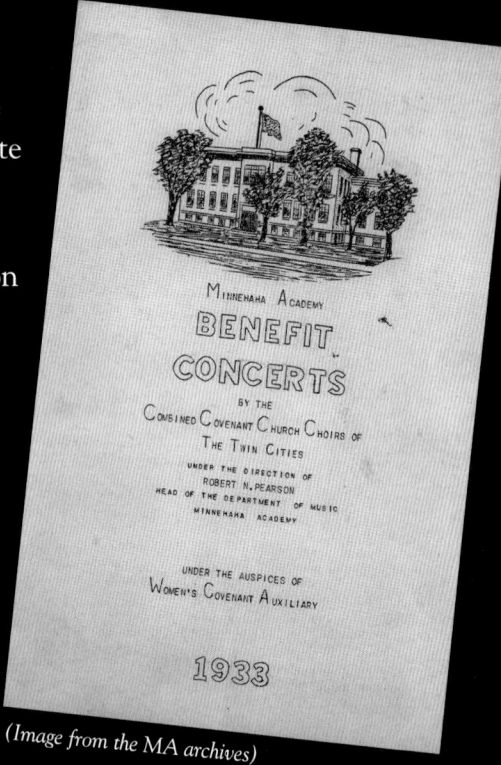

(Image from the MA archives)

(Image from the MA archives)

The Minnehaha Academy Women's Committee was first organized as the Women's Committee for Phase II of the Minnehaha Capital Funds Campaign in the 1970s. Phase II sought to raise $1,000,000 from the general community outside the Covenant Church for the new construction and remodeling of the school. As part of their fundraising efforts, the Women's Committee held their first annual holiday house tour in 1973, which became an annual tradition for many years. Other events sponsored by the Women's Committee have included a style show and luncheon started in 1979 and a spring flower sale called the "Best Blooming Sale Ever," held in the school's South Campus ice arena, beginning in 1987. In 1997, the Women's Committee changed its name to the MA Alliance, inviting women and men who were parents, grandparents, alumni, and friends of the school to volunteer for major fundraising events.

In 1974, the Women's Committee organized a two-day "Garage Walk" involving ten garages selling donated items and baked goods. After the purchase of the South Campus from Breck in 1981, the Women's Committee held its first official Arena Sale in the newly acquired hockey arena in 1984. The Arena Sale is one of the school's largest fundraising events that still continues today.

(Photos from the MA archives)

The Academy held its first Benefit Auction and Dinner in 1983. This was a major fundraising event to benefit the Academy's capital fund, and has always had a unique festive theme. Pictured are Alumni and Parent Relations Manager Jane Anfang and Director of Planned Giving Gayle Gilreath at the 2011 auction, which celebrated the royal wedding of Prince William and Kate Middleton.

(Photo from the MA archives)

1940–1949

(Photos courtesy of Jim Nash)

46 MINNEHAHA ACADEMY: A CENTURY OF FAITH AND LEARNING

MINNEHAHA ACADEMY grew significantly throughout the 1940s, with the most increases from 1943 to 1946, in the midst of America's involvement in World War II. The greatest increase of students occurred in the High School Department. Enrollment in the Bible Institute decreased in 1945 when men went to serve in the armed forces, resulting in the institute's temporary suspension. An attempt was made to reopen it in 1949 without success. As in the 1920s, the large jump in enrollment necessitated an expansion of the school's facilities. The Northwest-Minnehaha Advance Campaign was launched in cooperation with the Northwest Conference in 1946 and completed in 1949. In addition to the expansions of the student body and the school building, the faculty also doubled from twelve teachers to twenty-four in 1945 to keep pace with the school's growth. By the end of the decade the staff numbered thirty, three times the size of what it was in the 1930s.

Reverend Clarence A. Nelson became Minnehaha Academy's third president during World War II. He was a graduate of Minnehaha Academy from the class of 1918 and had served as pastor of Salem Covenant Church in Minneapolis, where he had begun and taught a teacher-training class.

(Photo from the MA archives)

He launched the Northwest-Minnehaha Advance Campaign from 1946 to 1949. Enrollment also expanded under his leadership from about 200 students to about 500 students.

Lawrence Bengtson was a veteran of World War II who began as a teacher of social studies at Minnehaha Academy in 1946. He became assistant principal in 1948 and principal in 1951. He studied at North Park College for two years before transferring to the University of Minnesota, where he received his Bachelor of Arts degree. After serving in World War II, he received his master's degree from the University of Minnesota. He continued to teach social studies from 1968 to 1973.

(Photo from the MA archives)

(Photo from the MA archives)

Arlene Anderson began teaching at Minnehaha Academy in 1945. She earned her bachelor's degree in history, English, and economics from Carroll College in Maukesha, Wisconsin, and a master's degree in educational administration, curriculum, and instruction from the University of Minnesota. She first taught in the public schools of Kingsford, Michigan. She came to Minnehaha after a brief experience in the federal government's Child Care Center in Minneapolis. She taught American history for four years, took time off to be an at-home mother, and returned to teach English. She also worked as an attendance counselor and managed the school's bookstore. In 1963, she became dean of students and later dean of instruction in 1967. When Minnehaha Academy acquired its South Campus, Anderson became its principal. She retired in 1984. After her retirement she remained involved in Minnehaha Academy, serving on the Minnehaha school board and becoming its chair in 1998.

(Photo from the MA archives)

Elwood (Woody) Lindberg started at the Academy in 1947. He served as athletic director and guidance counselor and taught social science until 1964.

(Photo from the MA archives)

Martha Pearson was a teacher of history for twenty years at Minnehaha Academy. She retired at the end of the school year in 1969. All three of her children were graduates of the Academy.

48 MINNEHAHA ACADEMY: A CENTURY OF FAITH AND LEARNING

Phyllis M. Englund taught English and German from 1948 to 1970. She also co-wrote *Forty Years in Faith*, a history of the school, with Gertrude A. Sandberg.

(Photo from the MA archives)

(Photo from the MA archives)

(Photo from the MA archives)

Harry P. Opel became head of the Music Department following Robert N. Pearson's sudden passing. Opel was a veteran of World War II and had joined Minnehaha Academy's faculty in 1948 as a teacher of psychology and instructor of voice. Opel taught music at Minnehaha Academy for thirty-seven years, retiring in 1985.

Paul G. Gjesdahl was a professor of chemistry and physics and registrar at the school from 1943 to 1962. In 1959, he was named one of the three best high school chemistry teachers in the state by the American Chemical Society. He suffered a stroke that caused him to lose his speech and died on December 15, 1968. His two children were graduates of Minnehaha.

Evangeline Peterson was a graduate of Gustavus Adolphus College. She also studied at the University of Minnesota. Prior to joining the Academy faculty, she taught at Cumberland, Wisconsin; Triumph, Minnesota; and Eagle Bend, Minnesota. She joined Minnehaha's faculty in 1943, teaching Latin and serving as the school's librarian for thirty-three years. She retired in 1977.

Adelyn Berg taught at Minnehaha Academy for twenty-seven years. She came to the school in the fall of 1948 from New York Mills, Minnesota. Berg graduated from Bethany College in Lindsborg, Kansas, with a major in English and business. At Minnehaha, she began by teaching English to freshmen and sophomores. After nine years she started teaching typing, bookkeeping, and elective subjects. Berg retired in June 1975.

(Photo from the MA archives)

Charles (Chuck) Sulack came to Minnehaha in 1948. He taught physical education and industrial arts and was head basketball coach for fourteen years. Sulack became athletic director in 1962. He left Minnehaha in 1968 to teach in the Industrial Arts Department at Kennedy High School in Bloomington, Minnesota.

(Photo from the MA archives)

1940–1949 49

WAR HITS HOME

President E. O. Franklin left his position as president in 1943 to serve as an Army chaplain until 1946. Principal Joseph R. Adell also resigned in 1943. The vacancies of the school's top two positions caused concern for some that the school might close due to lack of leadership, but Anna Fellroth became the school's principal and Reverend Clarence A. Nelson was selected as Minnehaha Academy's third president in 1943.

The 1944 *Antler* was dedicated to twelve classmates who left school to serve in World War II.

In addition to changes in leadership, the 1940s also brought several new additions to the curriculum. Following the trends of other local high schools to establish courses related to the increasing importance of peacetime and military aeronautics, the Academy introduced a Pre-Aviation course, which taught aerial navigation with an emphasis on the history of aviation and the study of the physical, mechanical, and atmospheric principles involved. Home economics first appeared as part of the curriculum in 1942. Ruth Reedholm was the school's first home economics teacher, though she only taught at the Academy for a year. The course initially taught cooking and sewing but expanded to include interior design and a class called Adult Living which taught skills for independent living, such as how to budget for rent and food, own and operate a used car, and live with a family.

To Our Classmates . . .

who have gone from our midst to heed the call of their country during this time of crisis, who have so willingly left their home, their church, and their school to preserve the justice, equality, and freedom for which America stands . . . we, the staff of 1944, do gratefully dedicate this Antler.

(Image from the MA archives)

Industrial arts, led by Charles Sulack, was added to the curriculum in 1948. Previously, Sulack had served as instructor for three years at the Naval Air Technical Training Center in Chicago. Because the school had no shop for industrial arts when it first began, a temporary space was provided in the boiler room. When a new gymnasium was added two years later, the class was held in an available space under the bleachers. The space included a wood shop, a drafting room, and a print shop (Nordstrom 2001, 140).

(Photo courtesy of Gerald Nordstrom)

50 MINNEHAHA ACADEMY: A CENTURY OF FAITH AND LEARNING

AN ASSOCIATION OF THEIR OWN

Minnehaha athletics continued to expand. In 1944, the Girls' Athletic Association was formed to allow more opportunities for girls to take part in sports. The association operated on a point system whereby each member could obtain a letter by earning points from participating in activities both in and out of school such as baseball, basketball, hiking, bowling, skating, archery, and a variety of other sports.

Bonnie Addington, class of 1947 and editor of the *Antler*, donated a scrapbook to the archives containing published and unpublished photos of early athletics and school life.

A school track team and hockey team were organized. The Academy also began to compete in an official league, the Minnesota State Private School League, consisting of Pillsbury Academy, Concordia, Shattuck Military Academy, Breck, and Minnehaha Academy. Minnehaha Academy's 1947–1948 boys' basketball team became the undisputed champion of the league.

In 1947, the school's six-man football team was converted to an eleven-man format following the growth of enrollment. The Academy's 1948–1949 boys' football team became undefeated champion in the Minnesota State Private School League, scoring 128 points against 19 during the season.

(Photos courtesy of Bonnie Addington)

(Photo from the MA archives)

1940–1949 51

A FEW FIRSTS OF THE 1940s

- Outside the classroom the school held its first Snow Day Carnival in 1947. Events of the day included skiing and tobogganing at the Town and Country Club, a hockey game, dinner, an alumni basketball game, and the crowning of the Snow Day royalty.

(Photo from the MA archives)

- In 1949, representatives for Girls' and Boys' State were chosen from Minnehaha Academy for the first time. This program, sponsored by the American Legion and American Legion Auxiliary, gave students an opportunity to learn about local, county, and state government and gain leadership skills through mock government exercises, which included electing representatives and enacting legislation. Eligible students had to be juniors in the upper third academic standing of their class, possessing good health and good character.

- The Board of Education organized a Parents and Teachers Association.

AROUND CAMPUS

The Minnehaha Singers continued to host sold-out concerts. In 1946, the Singers presented concerts of sacred and secular music with the African-American quartet, the Southernaires. During the concerts, William Edmondson of the Southernaires gave exhortations to racial unity.

Streetcar services were still in operation, though fares were increased to eleven cents per token in 1948. The school's Educational Council sent a letter to the Railroad and Warehouse Commission requesting that special consideration be given to students in the matter of transportation costs, but state laws prohibited discrimination in fares.

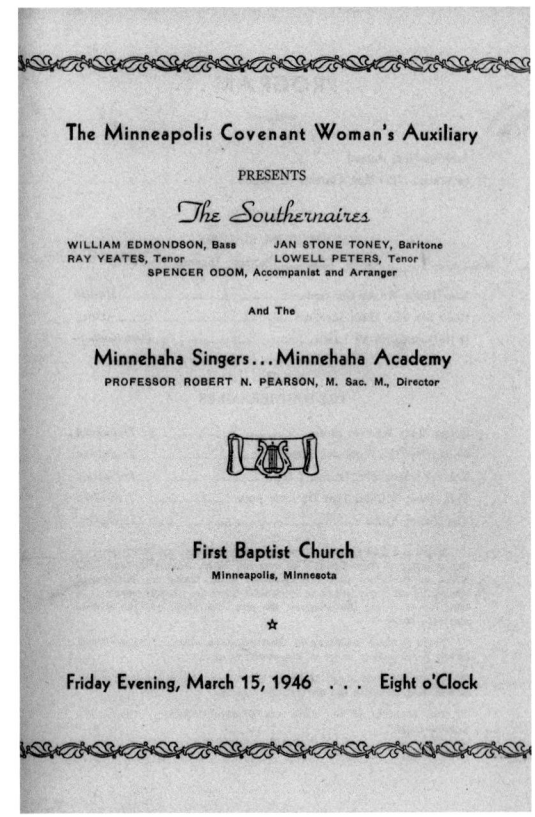

(Image from the MA archives)

(Photos courtesy of Bonnie Addington)

52 MINNEHAHA ACADEMY: A CENTURY OF FAITH AND LEARNING

IF THESE FLOORBOARDS
COULD SPEAK...

PROFESSOR PEARSON passed away suddenly on January 13, 1949. The last program he directed was the school's Christmas program where he led the Choristers, consisting of the Singers, Choir, and Chorus (approximately 250 voices in all), in the Hallelujah Chorus from Handel's *Messiah*, of which it was said in the May 1949 *Minnehaha Alumni News*, "it was so appropriate that he should leave us on the high and triumphant note, for there was no defeat nor retreat in his death" (*Minnehaha Alumni News*, Vol. III, No. 1, May 1949). Pearson's funeral was held on January 17, 1949. Students and faculty shared memories of him in the January 27, 1949 *Quiver*:

"It is hard to express in words what we feel towards our dear beloved Prof. The last time most of the kids saw him, was at the Christmas program standing so straight and tall and directing the Singers and Choirs beautifully. It seemed as though Prof directed more wonderfully than ever before."
—Betty Peterson '45

"My last memory of Prof occurred just before Christmas vacation. He had called three of us into his room, and we not knowing why, were rather curious about it. As it turned out, he just wanted us to decorate his room in a Christmas spirit. I can still remember him as he ran around getting and putting things up with the rest of us, enjoying himself just like everyone else."
—Ethel Nordstrom '50

(Photo courtesy of Bonnie Addington)

"We always had rare experiences on the busses. I recall the trip home from St. Olaf last spring. Before he had left home he was reminded by Pauline about the eggs, so he stopped both busses by this very modest farm house. He and Bill Busse went in to get the eggs while the rest of the Singers serenaded him with 'Because.' We were always reminded of his sense of humor. He reminded the Singers the next day that the eggs were very good."
—Marilyn Hanson '49

"Before Prof directed the Singers in a concert, he always looked down at his feet, it may have been to see if his podium was solid, but I believe it was to pray and ask God's blessing on the concert."
—Milton Quiqqle '50

"I remember how he directed us in choir, using a chair leg. We never knew when he'd sneak up behind us and bang it down on our chairs or even our heads."
—Arlene Strandberg '50

"Now that he has gone we hold pleasant memories of him in our hearts, and want to go on singing as though he were still here."
—Eunice Johnson '49

Professor Pearson formed string and brass ensembles and vocal groups as well as the Minnehaha Choir in the 1940s. He also directed the Minnehaha Band, which played during football and basketball games and pep fests.

Minnehaha Academy once ran several schools and programs that had to be discontinued for various reasons. The following is a brief overview of some of these disappeared traditions.

Four years of Swedish were provided as a language elective in 1913. Two years of Swedish were required, however, for students of Swedish nationality. Swedish was discontinued by 1956, revived for several years during the 1980s, but then discontinued again due to budget restrictions and enrollment numbers.

Minnehaha Academy provided Evening and Night School, including a Preparatory Night School for Scandinavians in the 1910s. Evening and Night School were also provided in the Bible Institute. Lawrence Bengtson, dean of instruction, also initiated an adult Evening School in the 1960s.

(Photos courtesy of Jim Nash)

P. J. Edquist, the school's first janitor, founded the Minnehaha Academy Sunday School. Edquist and his wife first gave Bible lessons to neighborhood kids on their front porch, but the class grew too large, so Edquist was given permission to use school classrooms. By 1922, the Sunday School enrolled one hundred students taught by fifteen teachers. Edquist died on December 25, 1922. A few days after his passing, twenty-six people gathered to charter the new Bethlehem Covenant Church, still located only a few blocks from Minnehaha Academy.

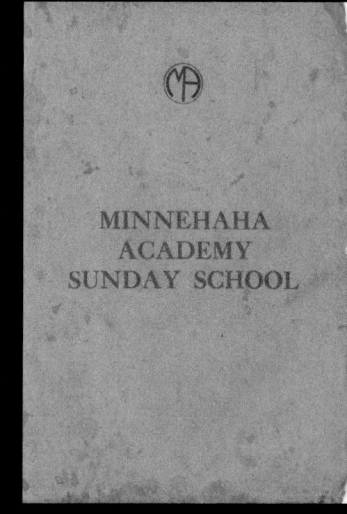

(Image from the MA archives)

The Minnehaha Academy Bible Institute opened on October 3, 1921. The motto of the Bible Institute was "The whole Christ/In the whole Bible/For the whole world." Students participated in Gospel Mission work, leading young people's services in Mission churches, visiting rest homes, shelters, and hospitals, and preaching in churches that had difficulty supporting a steady pastor. The first graduate of the institute, Helen Nelson Gravem, class of 1922, became a Covenant missionary to China. The Bible Institute continued until its official termination in June 1945 when the day school was closed, though courses in the evenings continued for several years after.

(Image from the MA archives)

On the flipside of programs phased out at Minnehaha Academy are those that were not a part of the school but are now staples of school life. Some of these activities were banned at one point, but allowed later after the bans were lifted, while others are the results of adopted changes in curriculum or culture.

(Images from the MA archives)

Many athletics were not officially organized and some were not even authorized by the school in the early decades. An excerpt from a 1921 *Quiver*, as quoted in the 1963 *Antler*, says, "A football has now been secured by the boys. Though playing football with other schools is forbidden, the boys are kicking the pigskin around every noon." The 1926–1927 Student Handbook also states, "In accordance with the rules in many other high schools, no girls' basket ball games with teams outside the school are permitted."

Drama was not allowed at Minnehaha Academy until 1952. The first play to be presented was a three-act play called *Melody*, described by its director, Zella Mae Sandin, as "a terrible play, but... a safe play for Minnehaha to produce" (Nordstrom 2010, 159).

In January 1990, Minnehaha Academy's Board of Education accepted the possibility of school-sponsored dances. Dancing had previously been banned from school-sponsored functions. The school board did approve square-dancing at the Sadie Hawkins in 1972 and other forms of folk dances were allowed as part of the language clubs' social events; however, these were viewed differently from contemporary social dancing. In March 1990, the board agreed to a set of guidelines for school-sponsored dances, and that spring the school held its first prom that allowed dancing. The Homecoming weekend of 1991 ended with the first-ever on-campus school dance, held in the North Campus gym.

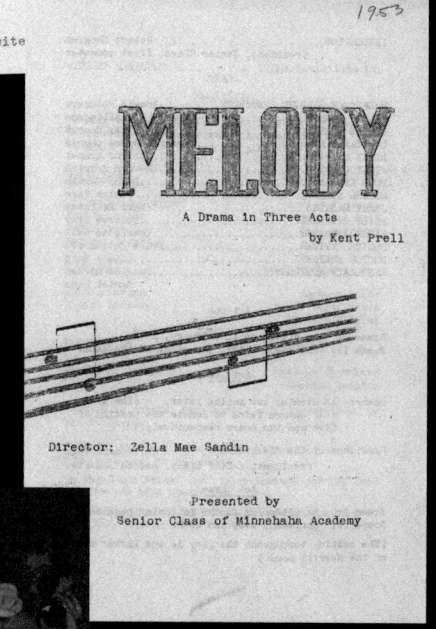

(Photo from the MA archives)

1950–1959

(Photos courtesy of Jim Nash)

56 Minnehaha Academy: A Century of Faith and Learning

THE STUDENT BODY reached its highest numbers ever of 500 students in 1949–1950. The recently completed expansion to the school increased its capacity, allowing for seventy-five more students. President Clarence Nelson left the Academy mid-year in 1949 to become president of North Park College and Theological Seminary. Arthur A. Anderson served as acting president following Nelson's departure, and then became the school's fourth president in 1950. The school continued to carry a large debt in the 1950s as a result of the construction in the late 1940s. Though the previous $300,000 goal of the Northwest-Minnehaha Advance Campaign had been exceeded, increased building costs and unanticipated repairs resulted in a school debt of $150,000. The school had to borrow from its current operating expenses to cover the monthly installments on this debt. The Carry On for Christ Campaign was launched in November 1952 to raise $300,000. Half of the money raised was to eliminate the Academy's debt and half was to be used by the Northwest Conference.

(Photo from the MA archives)

Arthur W. Anderson became president of the school in 1950. Anderson had completed seminary in 1946 and was invited by Nelson to be dean of boys and to teach Bible at Minnehaha Academy. Anderson was responsible for raising money to pay off a mortgage on the school construction and remodeling completed in 1949. He also led the framing of a statement of educational philosophy for the school.

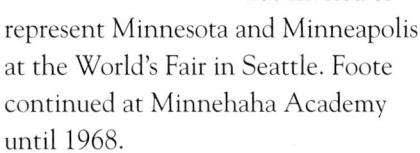

Lelia Foote was hired to take over the Academy's band in 1957. Foote promoted a concert band and introduced a series of popular mid-winter pop concerts. In 1962, Foote's concert band was invited to represent Minnesota and Minneapolis at the World's Fair in Seattle. Foote continued at Minnehaha Academy until 1968.

(Photo from the MA archives)

"Herr" Guido Kauls came to Minnehaha Academy in 1957 to teach German. Kauls introduced soccer to MA, organizing one of the first high school teams in Minnesota in 1961.

(Photo from the MA archives)

Kauls also initiated the Amity Scholars program at Minnehaha Academy in 1967. Kauls also met his wife Ann at MA. Ann was the daughter of former acting president Nathaniel Franklin. At the time of his retirement in June 2001, Kauls had taught for forty-four years, longer than anyone else in the school's history, and had coached soccer longer than anyone else in Minnesota at 894 soccer games.

(Photo from the MA archives)

Clarice Danielson taught French, English, and Latin at the Academy for twenty-two years. She also served as advisor for the *Antler*. She graduated from Augsburg College and pursued graduate studies at the University of Minnesota and the University of Wisconsin. Danielson retired in June 1975.

Gerald (Jerry) Nordstrom taught English, art, and theater at Minnehaha Academy for thirty-four years. He was the director of more than fifty plays and musicals. He also wrote *Where Youth Meets Truth: A History of Minnehaha Academy*, published in 2001. Nordstrom retired in 1993.

(Photo from the MA archives)

Willis Olson taught biology, Bible, and German at the Academy from 1953 to 1982. He also occasionally played the organ for school convocations.

(Photo from the MA archives)

58 Minnehaha Academy: A Century of Faith and Learning

A PRESIDENTIAL WEDDING

President Anderson was married on August 15, 1952. He and his wife moved into the president's house at 3106 47th Avenue S, Minneapolis, in 1953. The house was newly renovated as part of a general remodeling program which included replacing plumbing fixtures under the basement floor of Old Main, painting and beautification of all the school buildings, remodeling of the school laboratory, and landscaping the front campus. The PTA was active in raising money for these projects.

CHANGING OF THE GUARD

Two longtime teachers, Gertrude Sandberg and Sella V. Nelson, retired together in 1952. Alumni were asked to contribute toward the purchase of two round-trip train tickets to Miami, Florida, as a token of appreciation for the teachers' service. On the night of the PTA meeting when the tickets were going to be presented, neither of the teachers showed up. President Anderson personally delivered the tickets to them the next day. Sandberg and Nelson then went shopping for summer clothes, but because it was the middle of winter in Minnesota, they had a hard time finding anything available. During their trip down to Florida, they stopped in Chicago, where they were received by Reverend Clarence A. Nelson on the North Park College campus. Nelson invited Minnehaha alumni living in Chicago to his home for a reception for the two teachers. Sandberg and Nelson finally arrived at the Covenant Palms, where they spent the next six weeks on a hard-earned vacation (*Covenant Weekly*, Friday, February 13, 1953).

HOMEMAKER OF TOMORROW

Senior girls had a chance to earn a unique scholarship—the All-American Homemaker of Tomorrow offered by Betty Crocker. General Mills launched the program in January 1955. The scholarship involved a written exam that tested girls on many aspects of the "forgotten career" of homemaking, including family relationships, spiritual and moral values, child development, health and safety, money management, use of leisure time, home care, and more. All girls who took the test received a copy of *Betty Crocker's Guide of the Greatest Career in the World*. The Homemaker of Tomorrow from each school received a "Betty Crocker Award Pin." The state Homemaker of Tomorrow received a $1,500 scholarship, and the national All-American Homemaker received a $5,000 scholarship and a three-month tour of the United States.

MINNESOTA INDEPENDENT SCHOOL LEAGUE

The early 1950s were big years for Minnehaha Academy sports. In 1950, the basketball and hockey teams were Minnesota Private School League (MPSL) champions. In 1959, the basketball team won its tenth league championship in twelve years. In the fall of 1951, the football team became the last champions of the Minnesota Private School League which, with the additions of Blake and St. Paul Academy, was renamed the Minnesota Independent School League on December 6, 1951. The baseball team also won its third straight league championship the same year. Wrestling began to organize as a school sport in the later years of the 1950s.

The first meeting of the Lettermen's Club was held on November 6, 1956. One of the first things decided on was to purchase matching jackets, which were red wool with tan leather sleeves. Wrinkles the bulldog was the official mascot of the group, described in the 1956 *Antler* as "probably the ugliest yet friendliest dog ever to come to Minnehaha."

(Photo from the MA archives)

60   MINNEHAHA ACADEMY: A CENTURY OF FAITH AND LEARNING

SPIRITUAL LIFE REVIVAL

A number of new developments enhanced the spiritual life of the Academy in the 1950s.

In an effort to improve the effectiveness of the Student Council, a constitution was drafted to more clearly define the role of student government in the school. The government included an Ethics Committee focused on the conduct of students, a Religious Council providing leadership of religious life at the school, a Welfare Committee to remember students who became ill for extended periods and homes where a loved one passed away, an Assembly Committee which planned the Wednesday secular assembly, a Junior Red Cross Council to promote the purposes of the Red Cross, and a Social Committee to promote all school activities.

(Photo from the MA archives)

The Christian Service Club, counting upwards of one hundred members, was started to encourage Christian service through worship, music, and testimony. A few of the service projects that the club undertook included visiting children at the Shriner's Hospital for Crippled Children, singing for recovering polio victims at the Sister Kenny Institute, visiting with residents of the Bethany Old People's Home, and caroling for travelers around the Christmas tree at the Great Northern Railway Station.

A new altar made of oak was installed in the chapel to enhance the atmosphere of the Tuesday and Friday worship services. The altar was built so that it could be folded back and curtains could be drawn across it during the other days of the week. The altar was furnished with an open Bible and candelabras. Money for the altar was given in memory of Mrs. Eng Olson.

(Photo from the MA archives)

ONCE I WAS LOST, NOW I'M IN THE LOST AND FOUND

"'Thy word have I hid in the Bookstore' would be the way Minnehaha students would have to translate Psalm 119:11.

"If you have ever lost something and Mrs. Anderson can't find it, tell her to look under the pile of Bibles. Every day Bibles are turned into the lost and found, but no one ever claims them.

"Why is this? Have our students hid their Bible in their hearts by memorizing it all? I doubt it. If you have lost your Bible, its [sic] worth the nickel you pay to get it back."

(*Quiver*, December 1955)

A FEW FIRSTS OF THE 1950s

- The Minnehaha chapter of the National Honor Society started in 1954.

(Photo courtesy of Jim Nash)

- Art was first offered on a regular basis at the Academy in 1959. The subject was taught by a part-time teacher, which became a full-time position in 1966 (Nordstrom 2001, 164). Spanish was also added to the curriculum in 1957.

- Zella Mae Sandin taught English, Speech, and psychology from 1951 to 1964 and from 1967 to 1968. Sandin also directed *Melody*, the first play the school ever produced.

AROUND CAMPUS

Minnehaha Academy celebrated its fortieth anniversary in 1953. The Evangelical Mission Covenant held its sixty-eighth annual conference at the school June 17–21, 1953. The school published an anniversary book, *Forty Years in Faith*, written by MA teachers Phyllis M. Englund and Gertrude A. Sandberg, documenting the school's history to that point.

Students had fun with a library textbook from 1950. Inclusion of these photos is not in any way an endorsement of vandalism by the author of this book or the school. Defacing school property has always been prohibited. However, for those students who would still consider committing such a crime, it would be useful to bear in mind that the punishment for doing so might be less severe if the graffiti is rather clever.

(Image from the MA archives)

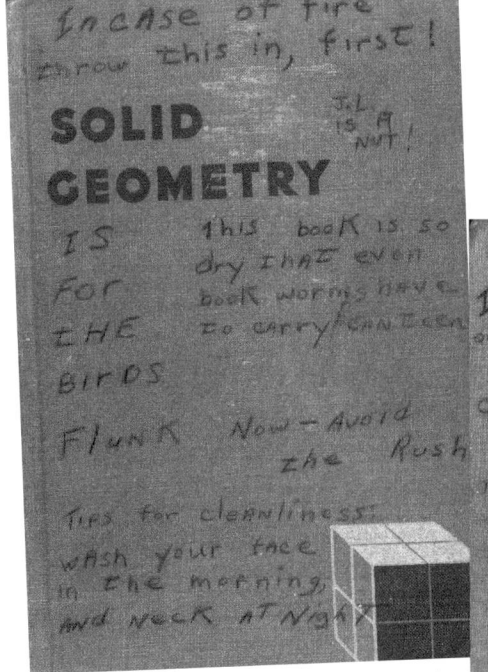

(Images from the MA archives)

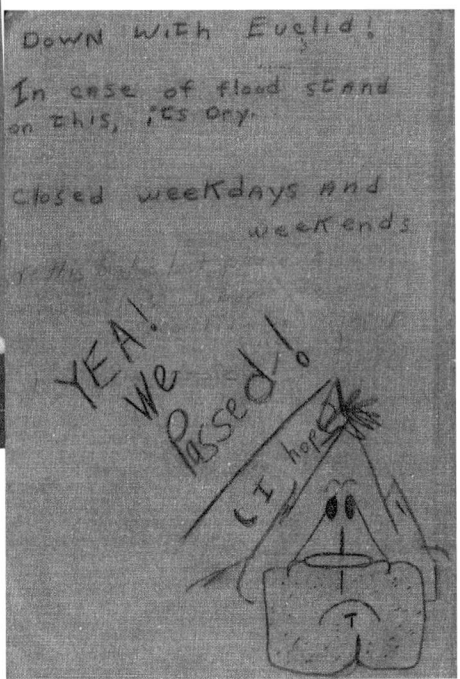

62 MINNEHAHA ACADEMY: A CENTURY OF FAITH AND LEARNING

IF THESE FLOORBOARDS
COULD SPEAK...

"IT IS POSSIBLE TO LIVE THROUGH AN ATOM BOMB RAID!" So exhorted the Student Handbooks of the 1950s as Civil Defense played its part at the Academy amidst the threat of nuclear attack.

"WHAT IS THE GREATEST CHALLENGE?"
BY AUSTIN EDMONDSON, JR.
FOOTBALL COACH

WHAT IS THE GREATEST CHALLENGE at Minnehaha Academy? Would you say it is preparing our students to go forth in the world and find their places in society; or would you say that since we have been ushered into a new era of Atom bombs and H-bombs, the more powerful and devastating bomb, we must prepare our students to survive in a world where it seems mankind is determined to destroy itself? Certainly these problems present great challenges to us, but I believe that the greatest challenge we have at Minnehaha Academy is to prepare our students with the saving knowledge of the word of God, enabling them to be a witness for the Lord in all things they do and say to the outside world, and show what the Lord himself can do through one who is willing to serve him in whatever walk of life he has chosen to follow....

(*Covenant Weekly*, September 18, 1953)

In addition to the instructions in the handbook, the private schools of the Twin Cities, including the Academy, cooperatively purchased the film *You Can Beat the Atom-Bomb*. The school also planned Civil Defense drills and discussed the installation of an air-raid warning system.

> by the door in each room. Acquaint yourself with these directions.
>
> 1. Keep in line. Walk rapidly, but do not run.
> 2. Do not talk until outside of the building.
> 3. The first two students out of any door will hold that door open until every one is out of the building.
> 4. Do not stop until at least 100 feet from the building.
> 5. Please do not stand in the area between the fire hydrant and the building.
>
> These matters are very serious. They might be a matter of life or death. To play with them or to play with the alarm equipment is considered a grave offense.
>
> CIVIL DEFENSE
>
> Upon receiving a yellow alert signal from the civil defense authorities, school will be dismissed by the principal. Students will be instructed to go home to be evacuated from the city according to plans made by each individual family. If going home means to cross the downtown area, the students should plan to leave the city immediately without going home. This is also true for those who will have no one home to meet them or who have no family transportation. City buses are assigned to transport students from the Academy who have no other means of transportation.
>
> In case of a red alert students are to seek the first available shelter. The best at school is found in the gymnasium building in the locker rooms, and also in the tunnels going to the shop. Most other areas afford only slight protection.
>
> SIX SURVIVAL SECRETS
>
> 1. Try to get shielded--stay away from windows.
> 2. Drop flat on the ground or floor.
> 3. Bury your face in your arms.
> 4. Don't rush outside right after a bombing.
> 5. Don't take chances with food or water in open containers.
> 6. Don't start rumors.
>
> The blast and heat are the two greatest dangers you face. The things that you do to protect yourself from these dangers usually will go a long way toward providing protection from the explosive radioactivity loosed by the atomic explosions.
>
> IT IS POSSIBLE TO LIVE THROUGH AN ATOM BOMB RAID!

(*Image from the MA archives*)

1950–1959

Minnehaha Academy's facilities have undergone extensive remodeling and additions to improve the school's services for expanding student enrollment and restore aged structures. The following is an overview of some of the Academy's most significant building campaigns.

The Thousand Tens Campaign was launched under the leadership of Reverend Nathaniel Franklin. The campaign raised $10,000 for the building's first addition, completed in 1916. The addition included expansions for the Business and Music departments as well as the construction of a residence for the president, located across from the school next to the current soccer field and now used as an office for the Northwest Conference.

(Photo from the MA archives)

The school launched its third building campaign in 1921, raising $100,000—the largest amount ever raised in the Covenant denomination at the time. This expansion added an entirely separate auditorium/gymnasium building, doubling the school's capacity. The new building was disconnected from the 1912/1916 building. A. L. Skoog laid the addition's cornerstone.

The Northwest-Minnehaha Advance Campaign was launched in 1946 under the leadership of Clarence A. Nelson to raise $300,000 for the school's fourth major building project and third addition to the original building. The expansion included construction of a new gymnasium, central annex, and remodeling of the 1922 building to include an indoor connection between the school's separate buildings.

(Photo from the MA archives)

The school's fifth major building program to construct a fine arts addition was launched in 1976. The fine arts addition was completed in 1977, expanding the available space of the Music, Art, and Industrial

(Photo from the MA archives)

Arts departments, adding a new stage to the existing gymnasium, and remodeling the old chapel/auditorium into a library. The old library became an audio-visual center. The school's heating system was also converted from stand-by coal to stand-by oil and forced air ventilation was added in the older school buildings.

(Photo from the MA archives)

(Photo from the MA archives)

The South Campus of Minnehaha Academy is located approximately one and a half miles south of the high school along the River Road in Minneapolis. Craig Nelson negotiated the purchase of the former Breck Campus facilities in 1981. The acquisition greatly expanded the Academy's capacity. The junior high program was moved to the South Campus, becoming a middle school program in the move. MA's lower school opened at the South Campus a year later.

Bloomington Campus opened as the Academy's first satellite campus in 1996. Bloomington offered lower-school classes (K-5) in the facilities of Bloomington Covenant Church. The Academy was able to open the campus due to a $1,000,000 gift, the largest single gift ever received by the Academy, from an anonymous donor in 1995 to start a satellite campus in the outer ring of the city. Bloomington Campus operated for fifteen years.

The Promise for the Future Campaign was launched in 2001. Planned renovations for the North Campus included a new three-court gymnasium, demolition of the old gymnasium to be replaced with a new chapel and performing arts auditorium seating 600, a new main entrance, two elevators, and more connections to existing buildings. The construction cost $15 million and was completed in 2003.

(Photo from the MA archives)

Following the North Campus expansion, the Foundation for a Lifetime Campaign of 2007 provided significant renovations to the South Campus, including a

(Photo from the MA archives)

350-seat chapel, classroom remodeling, modernizing the mechanical systems, updating the ice arena, improving parking, and modifying the exterior design to match the architectural look of the North Campus. The project cost $13.5 million and was completed in 2008.

(Photo from the MA archives)

1950–1959 65

1960–1969

(Photos courtesy of Jim Nash)

66 MINNEHAHA ACADEMY: A CENTURY OF FAITH AND LEARNING

Minnehaha Academy experienced a number of radical changes and reached a number of major landmarks in the 1960s. Arthur Anderson left the Academy to become chaplain at North Park College in 1959. Reverend A. Eldon Palmquist served as acting president from 1959 to 1960, until Wilbur M. Westerdahl became the school's fifth president in 1960. The school celebrated its fiftieth anniversary in 1963. The Academy also entered the computer age when Control Data donated a computer to the school—the first to be installed. With the addition of a computer, the school introduced Computer Programming as a course and a Computer Club was organized. Soccer became a major addition to the school's athletics. Enrollment also reached 641 in 1968–1969, which would be the highest figure ever for the Academy while it was still only a high school.

Reverend A. Eldon Palmquist, class of 1930, became acting president of Minnehaha Academy in 1959. Palmquist was the son of a pioneer Covenant pastor and an alumnus of Minnehaha Academy. While he was serving as active president, he was also pastor of the Edina Covenant Church. Reverend Wilbur M. Westerdahl succeeded Palmquist in 1960.

(Photo from the MA archives)

Reverend Wilbur M. Westerdahl became the school's fifth president in 1960. Westerdahl led the efforts to restore the school's regional accreditation of the North Central Association of Secondary Schools and Colleges, which had previously been dropped but was reinstated in 1965 following a two-year self-study.

Westerdahl also oversaw extensive renovations to improve the school's buildings, including the installation of a new electrical service, the installation of thermostats in every classroom, re-roofing, and the addition of a parking lot. Westerdahl also enhanced the fundraising of the school, re-established an Endowment Fund, and set up a Student Loan Fund during his administration.

(Photo from the MA archives)

Flora Sedgwick began teaching Honors English and speech at the Academy in 1960. She developed a nationally competitive and award-winning speech program at the school. Outside of the school day, she also introduced the first Advanced Placement course (English) to be offered at the Academy. In 1969, Sedgwick was given the Diamond Key Award, the highest given by the National Forensic League, for her work with the program's Minnehaha chapter. Sedgwick left Minnehaha Academy in 1971.

(Photo from the MA archives)

Wendell Carlson began his career at the Academy in 1963. He taught biology and life science and served as a drivers' education and audio-visual coordinator and as a counselor. He retired in 2006 after forty-three years.

(Photo from the MA archives)

Gordon L. Olson taught math, physics, chemistry, and computer science from 1967 to 1993.

(Photo from the MA archives)

David Glenn was an upper school social studies teacher who started at the Academy in 1966. He retired in 2008.

68 MINNEHAHA ACADEMY: A CENTURY OF FAITH AND LEARNING

Paul "Rabbi" Swanson was a graduate of Minnehaha Academy, class of 1951. He came from Alabama to attend the school. Swanson went on to North Park College, Western Reserve University, and North Park Seminary. He pastored churches in California, Alabama, and Michigan. He became a Bible teacher and chaplain at Minnehaha in the fall of 1966. Both of his parents, his wife, and his three children were also graduates. Swanson retired from full-time teaching in 2000, but returned to teach two classes in Honors Ethics.

(Photo from the MA archives)

David Lindmark began teaching at the Academy in the fall of 1968. He had studied at Northwestern College, served three years in the military, and graduated from the University of Minnesota. He taught tenth- and eleventh-grade English classes and coached three varsity sports: track and field, cross-country running, and Nordic skiing. He began the Nordic skiing program at Minnehaha in the late 1970s. He also started a summer outreach program, Great Expectations Ministries (GEM) fishing camps, in the late 1980s, combining Christian ministry with a passion for fishing. Lindmark retired in 2007 after thirty-nine years.

(Photo from the MA archives)

(Photo from the MA archives)

James (Jim) "Arrowhead" Erickson taught U.S. Social Studies from 1969 to 2005. Erickson was known for employing unique disciplinary measures for misbehaving students such as having them stick their foot in the garbage can or run laps around the school's parking lot.

(Photo from the MA archives)

Harvey Lundin was a teacher of math, computer programming, and chemistry and was a tennis coach. Lundin was known in part for being able to remove his shirt while still wearing his suit coat. He started teaching at Minnehaha in 1962 and retired in 1997.

(Photo from the MA archives)

Ted Malmsten was a math teacher who started at the Academy in 1966 and retired in 2000.

Virginia "Ma" Solvang began working in the school's office in 1969. In addition to managing attendance records, she also displayed senior pictures in her office and became Minnehaha Academy's lemon drop supplier when word of her personal stash got out. Two of her children attended Minnehaha. Solvang retired in the spring of 1992.

(Photo from the MA archives)

1960–1969 69

MODERNIZATION

The Academy began a modernization program in the 1960s. The modernization was made possible after the school was able to eliminate its building fund mortgage from the 1949 construction. In 1961, the spaces and equipment of the Home Economics, Chemistry, Physics, and Foreign Language departments were updated. The chemistry laboratory received new cupboards, offices for the faculty, and the addition of a fume hood to absorb fumes from experiments. The Covenant Women's Auxiliary raised $2,900 for the remodeling of the Home Economics Department. Four new kitchen units and a sewing unit were installed. In addition to physical improvements, the Academy sought to update its curriculum, introducing large group instruction in 1964 and strengthening the sacred studies courses by joining them with social studies courses.

As part of the modernization, the $12,500 Lingua Trainer Language Laboratory was installed in 1962 to assist with the teaching of foreign languages. The PTA and the class of 1961 both contributed toward its cost. The Language Lab consisted of thirty aqua booths and a master panel. From the master panel, as pictured with all the school's language teachers plugged in, the teacher could talk to an individual or to the entire class, arrange conversations among the students, and listen in on what they were saying. The students were able to record, listen to themselves talk, and talk to others.

(Photos from the MA archives)

70 MINNEHAHA ACADEMY: A CENTURY OF FAITH AND LEARNING

MINNEHAHA'S FLEET

In 1966, Minnehaha Academy began operating its own fleet of buses under the supervision of Richard Martinson. Martinson started the bus program with two buses. A third bus, a 1967 Chevrolet, was obtained through the Gold Bond trading stamps collected by Covenant Women—an effort led by Ellen Gustafson, also known as the "Stamp Lady," from Orono, Minnesota. Because the bus donated by the Covenant Women was paid for by Gold Bond trading stamps, the bill of sale states that the bus was purchased for "one dollar and other good and valuable considerations." The school's bus program grew from four vehicles with 120 riders to fourteen buses running twelve routes each school day for approximately 550 students at its height.

Harlon Hanson, seated on the steps of the bus, surrounded by the bus drivers for the school, came to Minnehaha in the fall of 1968 as transportation supervisor, responsible for managing the school's bus program. He retired in June 1984.

(Photo and image from the MA archives)

(Photo from the MA archives)

Richard Martinson began working at Minnehaha Academy on June 11, 1961, as supervisor of maintenance. Martinson began the school's bus program with two buses in 1966. Martinson was named director of operations in 1975–1976. Martinson's son Bradley, who graduated in 1977, became the first student to enter Minnehaha as an eighth-grader and stay through graduation. Martinson left Minnehaha in 1977 to take a position in a church in Redwood City, California.

(Photo from the MA archives)

1960–1969 71

A FEW FIRSTS OF THE 1960s

- The school hosted its first Sadie Hawkins party in 1965.

- A new prayer chapel was constructed in 1964. The Religious Council of the student government formally requested the space. Members of the school staff made the pews and the room.

(Photo from the MA archives)

- In addition to sponsoring fundraising concerts and plays, the PTA took on the project of re-decorating the school's lunchroom into a space that could provide both a lunchroom and student lounge in 1966. Thus the lunchroom became the Campus Room.

- The school introduced a new system of graduation honors: Highest Honors for students who maintained an average of 3.8 and above, High Honors students with averages between 3.6 and 3.8, and Honors for students with a 3.3 to 3.6 average. The change eliminated the traditional valedictorian and salutatorian designations, thereby awarding more credit to a greater number of students.

AROUND CAMPUS

(Photo from the MA archives)

Soccer became a major addition to the school's athletics. Minnehaha Academy produced one of the first high school soccer teams ever in the state of Minnesota. Guido Kauls organized and coached the team. Kauls came to Minnehaha Academy in 1957 to teach German. The first official soccer league was also formed. Five schools joined: Blake, Breck, Minnehaha Academy, St. Thomas Academy, and Shattuck. Minnehaha won the championship the first year. Kauls served as chairman of the Minnesota High School Soccer League from 1962 to 1966.

The Minnehaha Singers sang at an interfaith prayer service for the opening of the 1967 Minnesota legislature. The service was planned by the department of ecumenical relations of the Minnesota Council of Churches in cooperation with the Catholic Archdiocese of St. Paul and Minneapolis, the Eastern Orthodox Clergymen's Association, and the Minnesota Rabbinical Association.

(Photo from the MA archives)

IF THESE FLOORBOARDS
COULD SPEAK...

IN 1962, MINNEAPOLIS AQUATENNIAL QUEEN Pamela Jo Albinson invited Lelia Foote's concert band to represent Minnesota and Minneapolis at the World's Fair in Seattle, gaining national recognition for Ms. Foote, the Minnehaha Band, and the Academy:

"ACADEMY BAND HEADS FOR THE FAIR!"
BY WILLIAM H. GENTZ

[...] The Academy band was selected by the Minneapolis Aquatennial Association to be its representatives and accompany Queen of the Lakes Pamela Jo Albinson and Commodore Robert Gisselbeck at their World's Fair appearances. For the past three years the band has won top honors in its classification in Aquatennial competition and thus was a logical choice for the special Seattle trip.

One of the unusual aspects of this band is the fact its director is a woman. Miss Lelia Foote, a native of Hillsboro, Kansas, has led the band at Minnehaha Academy for the past five years. A lady band director in secondary schools is a real rarity; only one or two have ever gained national prominence. Miss Foote, who is being featured in a St. Paul Sunday newspaper story this month, attributes her success with the band to three things: "Prayer, hard work, and love."

Although she strives for musical excellence, Miss Foote believes that the attitude of the young musician is of first importance. Music is second to character, is her motto. [...]

At Minnehaha the band is an integral part of the whole process of Christian training. "'Teach a boy to blow a horn and he'll never blow a safe' is an old cliche," Miss Foote says, "but there is a lot of truth in it, nevertheless." [...]

(*Covenant Companion*, June 15, 1962)

In addition to playing for President Eisenhower in 1960, Lelia Foote's band was invited by Pamela Jo Albinson (pictured between Foote on the left and President Westerdahl on the right) to play at the World's Fair in Seattle. Foote received an official invitation signed by the president and commodore of the Minneapolis Aquatennial Association.

(*Photo and image from the MA archives*)

FOUNDATION OF FAITH

Attendance at chapel services has been required of Minnehaha Academy students since the very beginning. Though this tradition has endured for one hundred years, the look and feel of the school's chapel settings have undergone significant changes.

In addition to attending chapel services, students who came to the Academy in the earliest decades were also expected to attend worship on Sundays, at the church of their or their parents' choosing.

(Photo from the MA archives)

After the auditorium/gymnasium building addition was constructed in 1922, chapel was held in the auditorium.

(Photo from the MA archives)

Following the remodeling of the 1949 Northwest-Minnehaha Advance Campaign, chapel was held in the top floor of what is now the library until 1977.

(Photo from the MA archives)

During the construction of the fine arts addition in 1976, chapel time became a gathering of small groups in homerooms or chapels conducted over the school's new public address system, meetings of class groups, and worshiping as an entire student body once a week in the gym. Moveable bleachers with backrests were installed in the new gym for chapel services. Chapel would be held in the gym until the completion of the construction in the 2000s.

(Photo from the MA archives)

With the purchase of the school's South Campus, chapels were held for the lower and middle schools in the basement. Renovations of the North Campus in 1987 created a new chapel arrangement—the old stage on the west side of the gym was carpeted, lights were added, and a new backdrop designed by Gerald Nordstrom was set up. The backdrop was mobile, displaying a religious theme for chapel services on one side and a school theme for sporting and other events on the opposite side.

(Photos from the MA archives)

(Photos from the MA archives)

The construction in the 2000s added a new chapel and performing arts auditorium seating 600 to the North Campus and a new 350-seat chapel to the South Campus.

1970–1979

(Photos courtesy of Jim Nash)

76 MINNEHAHA ACADEMY: A CENTURY OF FAITH AND LEARNING

Minnehaha Academy's halls swelled with the addition of a junior high program in 1972. **The school reached its highest enrollment levels in its history during the late 1970s, with all students crammed into the single North Campus building.** The class schedule consisted of nine periods of forty minutes each. The forty-minute periods were further divided into modules of twenty minutes, allowing sixty-minute periods for such classes as science laboratory, physical education, or home economics. In addition to reaching younger students, the school also sought to increase its financial aid to inner-city students. Faculty provided remedial teaching and tutorial sessions at local churches. The school launched its fifth major building program in 1976—a fine arts addition that was completed in 1977. Also in 1976, President Westerdahl returned to parish ministry in Redwood City, California. C. Allan Bodin became acting president from 1976 to 1977 and was relieved by Reverend Craig W. Nelson, who became the sixth president of Minnehaha Academy in 1977.

(Photo from the MA archives)

Mr. C. Allan Bodin, vice-chairman of the Board of Trustees, became acting president of Minnehaha Academy in 1976. While serving as acting president, he also continued part-time on the administrative staff of the Robinsdale School District. Bodin was relieved by Reverend Craig W. Nelson. In 1982, Nelson asked Bodin to return to Minnehaha Academy as vice-president and assist in the expansion that included a lower school on Minnehaha Academy's South Campus. Bodin was also put in charge of the school's bus service. Bodin, his wife, and their three children were all graduates of Minnehaha Academy.

(Photo from the MA archives)

Reverend Craig W. Nelson, son of former president Clarence A. Nelson, became the sixth president of Minnehaha Academy in 1977. Nelson was a graduate of Minnehaha Academy, class of 1949. He left his position as pastor of Bloomington Covenant Church to serve the school. Under his leadership the school eliminated its debt. Nelson also oversaw the acquisition of Minnehaha Academy's second campus, formerly belonging to Breck. Minnehaha Academy's new South Campus allowed for the addition of lower school classes, kindergarten through sixth grade, and student enrollment increased from 720 students to nearly 1,200.

(Photo from the MA archives)

Kenneth Greener began working at Minnehaha Academy in 1971, providing assistance to President Wilbur Westerdahl during the capital campaign. He moved into the position of dean of students, which he held until the addition of the South Campus in 1981, when he accepted the position of upper school principal. He also served as dean of instruction. Greener left MA in 1996.

(Photo from the MA archives)

Barb Olson taught English from 1973 to 1985 and returned as upper school principal from 1996 to 2001.

(Photo from the MA archives)

Janet Johnson is an upper school English teacher who started at the Academy in 1972.

(Photo from the MA archives)

David Hepburn taught instrumental music at the Academy from 1970 to 1979.

(Photo from the MA archives)

(Photo from the MA archives)

Kenneth (Ken) Anderson served as the school's athletic director from 1978 to 2011.

(Photo from the MA archives)

James (Jim) Wald, class of 1967, started teaching industrial arts at the Academy in 1971. Wald later took a position as plant manager and then director of finance and operations. He retired in 2012.

Carolyn Forsell began her teaching career teaching in Staples, Minnesota, for three years before becoming a substitute teacher at Minnehaha over the 1976–1977 school year. She then moved to El Paso, Texas, and taught at the Lydia Patterson Institute for three years. She earned her master's degree in English from Bemidji State in 1980 and in the fall returned to teach tenth-grade English and seventh-grade language arts at Minnehaha until her retirement in 2010.

(Photo from the MA archives)

(Photo from the MA archives)

Paul Norby began teaching Bible at the Academy from 1978 to 1981. From 1981 to 1994, he was assistant principal and taught AP History. From 1995 to 1999, he was administrative dean. He also held the position of admissions director until 2005.

Forrest Dahl is a middle school sacred studies teacher who started at the Academy in 1979. He has also been a tennis coach and has led chapel singing with his guitar.

(Photo from the MA archives)

Merry Mattson is the director of technology at Minnehaha Academy. She came to the school to teach computer science along with courses in business in 1979. In addition to teaching, Mattson has been instrumental in developing the Academy's technology infrastructure and has been recognized for her leadership and vision in improving education through the use of technology.

Mary Carlson is an upper school physical education, health, and sports medicine teacher who started at the Academy in 1972.

(Photo from the MA archives)

1970–1979 79

(Photo from the MA archives)

Geri DeVries taught English from 1972 to 2000.

(Photo from the MA archives)

Elaine Ekstedt, class of 1969, began teaching English at the Academy in 1973. She took over the school's publications program from 1976 to 1991, developing the publications class that produced both the *Antler* yearbook and the student newspaper. She also established the learning specialist position in 1991 and is currently director of special academic needs, an all-school position.

(Photo from the MA archives)

Wallace (Wally) Borner is a middle school social studies teacher who started at the Academy in 1974.

(Photo from the MA archives)

Sue McAllister was an upper school guidance and college counselor who served at the Academy from 1975 to 2010.

(Photo from the MA archives)

Phillip (Phil) Erickson is a middle school English teacher who started at the Academy in 1975.

Renee Troselius began as librarian of the North Campus in 1977. With the addition of the South Campus, she became the South Campus librarian for the lower and middle schools.

(Photo from the MA archives)

Evelyn Swanson began teaching at Minnehaha in 1976. She was an instructor of typing and shorthand, and transitioned to teaching computer applications and keyboarding. Swanson retired in 1997 but has continued on as a substitute and volunteer.

(Photo from the MA archives)

Theresa Lund worked in the school office from 1975 to 2006 and was in charge of purchasing for many years.

(Photo from the MA archives)

(Photos from the MA archives)

THE LEARNING CENTER

The construction of the fine arts addition in 1976–1977 converted the old chapel into a new Learning Center and library at the beginning of the building program. The Student Handbooks of the 1970s which described the Learning Center as "probably the nicest, but one of the least appreciated rooms in the school" now encouraged its use for quiet study and directed students to the Campus Room for group study, reflecting a shift from the earliest decades when any students not in class were required to be in the study room where they were not allowed to leave without a teacher's permission, were not allowed to study lessons in groups, and could only whisper to another student about matters pertaining to their lessons.

TRI-METRO CONFERENCE

In 1973, Minnehaha Academy, along with Blake, left the Minnesota Independent School League to join seven public schools in the newly formed Tri-Metro Conference. The schools included Brooklyn Center, Centennial, Mahtomedi, Golden Valley, St. Francis, Marshall University, and St. Anthony. The new conference was unique in that it included two private schools, five suburban public schools, one inner-city public school, and one rural public school. In 1974, Minnehaha joined the Minnesota State High School League (MSHSL). This allowed Minnehaha to participate in state tournaments and competitions with public schools as well as private schools.

(Photos from the MA archives)

Girls' track, tennis, cross-country, and volleyball were all introduced as organized sports in the 1970s.

A FEW FIRSTS OF THE 1970s

- *The Music Man* was the first full-scale musical production held in the renovated facility of the auditorium/gymnasium. Fine Arts Department faculty Gerald Nordstrom, David Hepburn, and Harry Opel directed the show. Nearly 3,000 people saw the production, presented by a cast of fifty-six and backed by a twenty-one-member orchestra. Dr. Ken Greener and Janet Johnson played the lead roles.

- In 1977, Guido Kauls organized and coached the first girls' soccer team at Minnehaha Academy, then one of only three girls' teams playing on a club level.

- The annual student art and literary publication, *Spirit*, was launched in 1973 and released annually. The last edition was published in 2004.

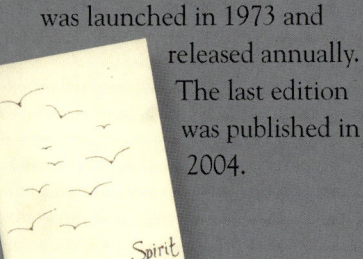

AROUND CAMPUS

The girls' basketball team coached by Mary Carlson won the school's first Tri-Metro Championship in 1974–1975. Jean Rhode, a senior, led the team as the leading scorer in the Tri-Metro Conference with 301 points for the season.

The school continued to find unique ways to raise money for its campaigns. On November 19–20, 1977, eighty-five Minnehaha students, parents, and friends rocked in rocking chairs for twenty-four hours, earning $10,000 in pledges. Many performance groups such as the New Song Singers and the Augsburg Jazz Ensemble entertained the rockers during the Rock-a-Thon event.

(Photo from the MA archives)

(Photos from the MA archives)

82 MINNEHAHA ACADEMY: A CENTURY OF FAITH AND LEARNING

If These Floorboards
could speak...

The following are a few excerpts of poetry written by junior high students published in the 1978 *Spirit* literary magazine:

"People"

People run and people walk
People sing and people talk

Same old pace every day
People just can't get away

People here and people there
People, people everywhere

Over and over every day
Watching their lifetime pass away

Cut down trees put up a store
People don't care about trees
  anymore

Who can stand this awful pace
As if we're running in a race

Must go fast can't go slow
But we need time and room to grow

People keep their feelings inside
Even if someone they love has died

People can't stop for even an hour
Or even a minute to look at a flower

Seconds, minutes and hours pass
Not even time to sit in the grass

People live and people die
Without even looking at the sky

People don't use their brains
  anymore
they go out and buy them at a store

People walk with eyes straight ahead
And stay that way until they're dead

People's fun is not satisfactory
Unless the fun is from a factory

People come and people go
People pass without hello

Who gives a hoot about an old
  alligator
People just want a new calculator

What cost a nickel now is a dollar
People can't whisper; they now have
  to holler

Prices are high and fuel low
But people still want to go, go, go

They say they can go faster than light
But have they ever looked up at the
  sky at night?

They say they're making better cars
But have they ever seen the stars?

Sean Krueger, grade 7
(*Spirit*, 1978)

"My Day as a Lightning Bolt"

I am striking on the earth
with my electric ray, flashing
my bright razor light on the
oncoming earth. I zig zag, bolting
with the speed of light, shrieking
with my thundering voice.

Larry Jaehnert, grade 7
(*Spirit*, 1978)

(Photos from the MA archives)

In 1972, a junior high program was added, expanding Minnehaha Academy's programming to the seventh and eighth grades. The school surveyed its community as part of the process to determine whether to add the grades. The addition made it possible for interested parents to send their children to Minnehaha Academy for the full six years of secondary education and also served to bring the school's programming more in line with the 6-3-3 organization of public schools.

Minnehaha Academy has made great strides in technology, strides that the founders of the school could probably never have imagined. Computer labs, electronic "blackboards," and MA on Facebook? These are just a few of the ways the Academy has kept up with the rapidly expanding influence of technology in schools. Though the technology of the early decades, such as mimeographs, delineascopes, or typewriters, might seem antiquarian today, even then the school was focused on providing the best, most current, and most effective tools for its students. Check out a few of the technological landmarks the school has established.

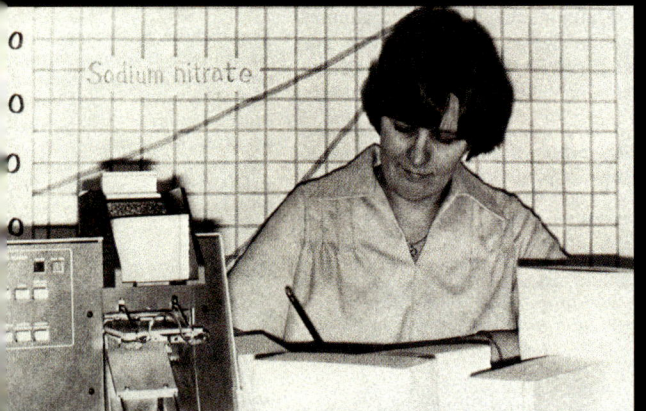

1967: Minnehaha Academy received a 1967 Bendix G15 computer—the school's first. The computer was donated by Bendix, which would later become Control Data. The computer used paper tape and contained 550 vacuum tubes. The machine took up an entire room, which had to be air-conditioned—another first for the school. Harvey Lundin oversaw the use of the computer.

(Photo from the MA archives)

1980: Under the terms of a federally funded program (Title IV) for the purchase of library and instructional materials and equipment, the school received a microcomputer for instructional use—an Apple II. Word processors and printers were also received from individual donations and through the Minnesota Independent School Fund, Inc.

1984: With the addition of more accessible computers, word processing and computer science were added to the school's curriculum. The school received gifts of two Remington Rand/Serif II word processors and printers from Mr. and Mrs. John F. Roy. The Academy also received a 3M Secretary III copier for use at the South Campus from 3M through the Minnesota Independent School Fund, Inc.

(Photo from the MA archives)

(Photo from the MA archives)

84   Minnehaha Academy: A Century of Faith and Learning

1995: The school established a new computer lab. All the computers in the lab were networked together and connected to a brand-new server. By December, the school had its very own T1 connection to the Internet, making it one of the first schools in the state to have a fast Internet connection directly linked to the school. The computers were also connected to the computers at the South Campus. The lab was made up of sixteen Macintosh computers, three PCs, and one brand-new Compaq Pentium server. The technology was managed by Merry Mattson and supported by Peter Jerde.

1996–1997: Merry Mattson and Rich Enderton received a mini-grant to travel to Texas where they designed the first webpages for the school. Since then, like the school's physical buildings, its virtual building (MinnehahaAcademy.net) has undergone significant changes over the years. In addition to its main website, the school launched Redhawks Online (redhawksonline.com) which stores digital archives of the student newspaper and yearbooks. The Academy is also now connected through social networks. If you're a technophile, you can follow MA on Facebook, accessible through the school's homepage.

(Photo from the MA archives)

2000s: Minnehaha Academy now uses SMART Boards, Promethean Boards, and additional components such as ActiVote, ActivExpression, and ActivSlate to enhance learning in classrooms. Interactive whiteboards are interactive displays that combine whiteboards with computers and projectors, allowing students or teachers to combine images, video, and audio with handwriting. ActiVote and ActivExpression are wireless devices that allow students in their seats to interact individually and as a class with the whiteboards. The school continues to seek ways to introduce the most current and relevant technology in its classrooms and will require iPads for all fifth- and sixth-grade students beginning at the start of the school year in 2012.

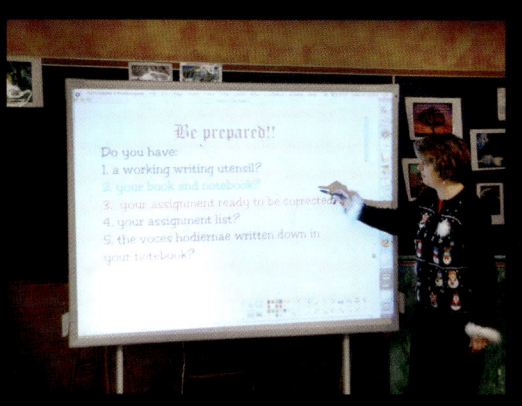

(Photo from the MA archives)

1980–1989

(Photos courtesy of Jim Nash)

The 1980s saw a peak in enrollment, topping 1,100 in 1986–1987, resulting in the largest graduating class ever with 195 students. In the summer of 1981, Minnehaha Academy purchased South Campus (formerly Breck School) and began a middle school program there. Because the South Campus facilities had superior science labs and equipment, chemistry and physics classes from the high school were bussed down during the day. Renovation of the North Campus in 1987 included the installation of a new, up-to-date science lab in the original 1913 building. The old science lab hadn't been changed since the 1920s, except for the addition of contemporary equipment. Enrollment began to drop, however, at the end of the 1980s. A smaller student population toward the end of the 1980s resulted in all seniors receiving their own lockers, which was a change from the former arrangement of three seniors sharing two lockers. The Academy's busing service, in operation since 1966, was discontinued in 1986, at which point the services of commercial bus companies were leased. Minneapolis students bussed free of charge for the first time.

(Photo from the MA archives)

Paul Osterlund became the first principal of the lower school on July 1, 1982. Osterlund received his Bachelor of Science in Elementary Education from the University in 1974 and a Master of Arts in Educational Administration from the University. He also earned his Specialist's Certificate in Educational Administration at the University of Minnesota in 1982.

(Photo from the MA archives)

Dean Erickson was a graduate of Minnehaha Academy, class of 1967. He served as principal of the middle school for twenty-five years before resigning to accept a position as superintendent of Meadow Creek Christian School in Andover, Minnesota.

(Photo from the MA archives)

Charice Deegan started at the Academy in 1988 and served as lower school principal and Summer Programs director. She also established an Extended Day Program at the South Campus in 1988.

(Photo from the MA archives)

Lance Johnson started at the Academy in 1984. He has taught lower school physical education, coached basketball, and held the position of upper school assistant principal. Johnson is currently the upper school dean of students and advisor for the student interns.

(Photo from the MA archives)

Paul Isaacs was a Mankato State University graduate. He joined the Academy's instrumental music faculty in 1980, teaching junior high general music and band and ninth-grade band. He also assisted with sectionals and small ensembles. Isaacs passed away from cancer on May 15, 2010.

(Photo from the MA archives)

Rich Enderton is an upper school math teacher who started at the Academy in 1982. Enderton has been nationally recognized for his teaching. He was selected as the 1992 National Educator of the Year by *Electronic Learning Magazine*. In 2000, Enderton received the Presidential Award for Excellence in Mathematics and Science Teaching, one of only four teachers in the state of Minnesota to be so honored.

(Photo from the MA archives)

Kathleen (Kathy) Johnson was a kindergarten teacher, lower school principal, director of development, and director of admissions. Johnson was also charged by President John Engstrom with starting the Bloomington Campus. She started at MA in 1985 and left in 2012.

Debora (Debbie) Fondell graduated from the University of Minnesota. She was a teaching aide at Lakeville Middle School in Minnesota before she joined the Minnehaha faculty in 1980 to teach recent American history and seventh-grade English. Fondell passed away from cancer on July 22, 2011.

(Photo from the MA archives)

Karen Wald came to Minnehaha in 1981 and began teaching middle school choir and general music, but spent most of her years teaching choir in the lower school. She retired in 2010 after twenty-nine years.

(Photo from the MA archives)

(Photo from the MA archives)

Gordon R. Olson took over leadership of Minnehaha's choral music program after the retirement of Harry Opel. Olson introduced the Madrigal Singers, which began the tradition of presenting an annual Madrigal Dinner. Olson retired in 1999.

(Photo from the MA archives)

Dan Bergstrom is an upper school chaplain and sacred studies teacher who started at the Academy in 1983.

Bonnie Morris is an upper school librarian who started at the Academy in 1982.

(Photo from the MA archives)

(Photo from the MA archives)

Carrie Johnson is a lower school elementary teacher who started at the Academy in 1982.

Daniel (Dan) Hauge is a middle school science teacher who started at the Academy in 1982. He has also coached wrestling.

(Photo from the MA archives)

Steve Engdahl is a middle school counselor who started at the Academy in 1982.

(Photo from the MA archives)

(Photo from the MA archives)
Willamae Swenson was the middle school dean of students from 1984 to 2004.

(Photo from the MA archives)
Cynthia McGovern launched the lower school art program in 1988. She taught at MA from 1988 to 2011.

(Photo from the MA archives)
Janet Peterson is the business manager. She started at the Academy in 1986.

(Photo from the MA archives)
Ruth Francis is a lower school technology teacher who started at the Academy in 1981. She has also been assistant librarian at the South Campus.

(Photo from the MA archives)
Nancy Greener taught first grade and fifth grade at Minnehaha for twenty-two years. All three of her children are graduates of Minnehaha. She retired in 2007.

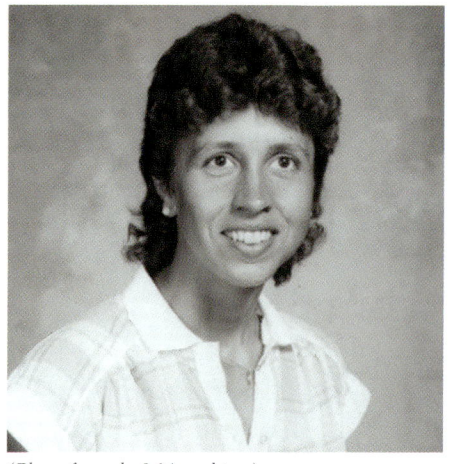

(Photo from the MA archives)
Katie Humason is a middle school science teacher who started at the Academy in 1985.

(Photo from the MA archives)
Dorothy Wintz was a middle school math teacher from 1981 to 1994 and 1999 to 2011.

(Photo from the MA archives)
Sandra (Sandy) Elhardt is a middle school physical education and health teacher who started at the Academy in 1983.

Curt Bjorlin started at the Academy in 1982 as a woodshop teacher. He is currently part of the school's operations staff.

(Photo from the MA archives)

90 MINNEHAHA ACADEMY: A CENTURY OF FAITH AND LEARNING

Dale Bengston is the grounds supervisor for the North and South campuses. He started at the Academy in 1984. 
(Photo from the MA archives)

Lorie Christianson is the media assistant for the North Campus library. She started at the Academy in 1983 as a mother volunteer and retired in 2012. 
(Photo from the MA archives)

(Photo from the MA archives)

Gloria Holmen, Ronna Capel, and Diane Thatcher. Both Gloria and Diane served MA for thirty years, and Gloria retired in the spring of 2012.

Lance Williamson was a custodian at the South Campus. He worked at the Academy from 1981 to 2008.

(Photo from the MA archives)

Stan Kne was a custodian at the South Campus. He worked at the Academy from 1981 to 2006.

(Photo from the MA archives)

Bruce Peterson is the ice arena and transportation director for the South Campus. He started at the Academy in 1982.

(Photo from the MA archives)

HARRY OPEL HONORED

In 1983, Harry Opel was honored by the American Choral Directors Association with its F. Melius Christiansen Memorial Award given to one outstanding choral director each year. In 1985, Governor Rudy Perpich issued a State of Minnesota Proclamation designating May 12, 1985 as Harry P. Opel Day for his work as choral director and his contributions as a soloist with the Bach Society, the Minnesota Orchestra, the Guthrie Theatre, and the Minneapolis Civic Orchestra (Nordstrom 2001, 92).

Bonnevieve Opel, class of 1932, was the wife of music director Harry Opel. She often played the organ as accompaniment during choral programs and also taught piano and organ from 1966 to 1985.

(Photos from the MA archives)

1980–1989 91

A FEW FIRSTS OF THE 1980s

- In 1986, computers (an Apple IIe and Brother printer) were used to produce the school's student publications, the *Quiver*, *Antler*, and *Spirit*, for the first time.

- The Cross Country Ski Club became a team for the first time.

- The Academy was one of the first schools in Minnesota to require community service for graduation. Starting in 1985–1986, seniors had to fulfill twenty-five hours of volunteer work to graduate.

- The boys' varsity tennis team, coached by Forrest Dahl, became Minnehaha Academy's first state champion team in 1986. Not only did MA win the team championship with wins over Edina and Stillwater, but Jason Hall was the champion and Ryan Skanse was runner-up in the individual state competition.

(Photo from the MA archives)

AROUND CAMPUS

Gordon Olson, who became director of the school's choral programs following Opel's retirement, introduced the Madrigal Singers, a group of sixteen juniors and seniors from the Singers who performed "madrigal" music, a style originating in Italy during the thirteenth and fourteenth centuries. Olson also started the elaborate production of the Madrigal Dinner, a Renaissance-themed Elizabethan musical feast, complete with full-course meals. The dinner was interspersed with performances by the Madrigal Singers, faculty King and Queen representatives, and jesters, monks, beggars, minstrels, and actors to entertain guests throughout the evening.

(Photo from the MA archives)

The F. J. Hollinbeck Memorial Library Fund was established in honor of Frank Justus Hollinbeck by his son and daughter-in-law, Richard Hollinbeck (class of 1925) and Ethel Lindell (class of 1928). Richard and Ethel donated the *Birds of America* four-volume double-elephant folio-size set in 1986. The set consists of a collection of paintings of life-size birds by John James Audubon. Audubon produced the paintings from 1827 to 1838. The school's copy is one of only 200 made of the original. It was valued at over $18,000 at the time of reception according to librarians Bonnie Morris and Lorie Christianson. The set is currently on display in the school's library, next to a bust of F. J. Hollinbeck created by Ethel.

(Photo courtesy of Jim Nash)

If These Floorboards
could speak...

The following are a few creative writing excerpts written by middle school students at the South Campus and published in the 1980s *Spirit* literary magazines:

"Toast"

Scrapy, crunchy,
Square, tinted
Rough, flaky
Wheaty, tasty
Fresh, grainy
As a great hot grain field
Breakfast would not have a thing to boast,
Without toast.

Elliot Graham, grade 7
(*Spirit*, 1981)

"Tacos"

Crunchy, munchy
Yellow, funny
Coarse, grainy
Graining, nummy
As a leafy sombrero,
I eat plenty as head-honcho.

Elliot Graham, grade 7
(*Spirit*, 1981)

A missile comes out of the sky.
A mushroom grows a thousand feet high.
They started this, I wonder why.
A few to live,
The rest to die.

Amy Simso, grade 8
(*Spirit*, 1984)

"Morning Stillness"

It is dawn, the air is cool and fresh
A light, soft mist covers a lake
Nothing stirs.
You are alone in a world refreshed by the night.

Mike Larose, grade 8
(*Spirit*, 1984)

"People"

No matter your color
No matter how tall
Just be what you are
And give it your all.

Dan Beasley, grade 8
(*Spirit*, 1984)

(Photos from the MA archives)

The Academy quickly expanded its programming beyond middle school following its purchase of the South Campus. In 1982, the lower school opened for students in grades one through five. In 1983, the South Campus further expanded its programming to include children down to age six. The first volume of the *MinneAntler*, the yearbook for the lower and middle schools, was also published. The Academy began a Summer School program again in 1983 at the South Campus and added a kindergarten to the school programming in 1985.

A NEW IDENTITY

Minnehaha Academy's mascot was the Indian for over seventy-five years, which is why the decision to change it in the late 1980s was no small affair. The school had to face the challenging process of choosing a new mascot that everyone could positively identify with and effectively communicate the reasons for the change to the student body.

The issue of school mascots bearing Native American names and symbols was not restricted to Minnehaha Academy. A broader social movement was expressed both on a national level concerning national football and baseball team names and on a local level concerning other high schools similar to the Academy. The Minnesota State Education Department encouraged all Minnesota schools at the time to eliminate Indian names as mascots.

In a letter to the Board of Education in 1988, president Craig W. Nelson wrote, "For many years Minnehaha Academy has used as its symbol (mascot) the 'Indian'. Over the years we have become increasingly aware of the necessity to treat this symbol with dignity and respect. During the past decade, while the Indian symbol has been treated respectfully by Minnehaha students and faculty, it has become increasingly apparent that its use caused concern in the Native American community. Last year the concern came to a head at Southwest High School, where finally under pressure, the symbol was changed. Minnehaha's administration has discussed for several years the use of the Indian symbol. This Spring we met with Mr. Philip St. John, a representative of the Native American community. He made us aware of the deep concerns in his community over the use and sometime misuse of this symbol. As a result of his presentation and our earlier discussions, the Administrative Committee decided to explore the changing of our symbol."

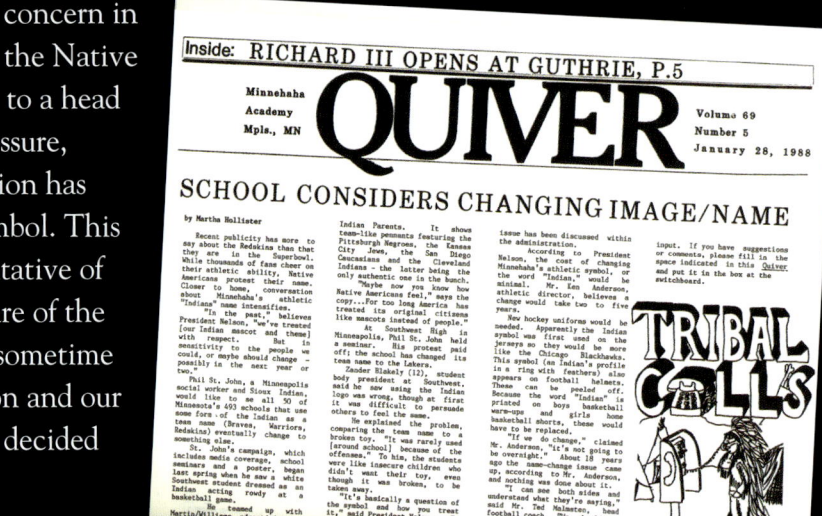

Following a vote by the faculty from the lower, middle, and upper schools, the results of which were fifty-six to change, ten abstaining, and two not to change, the decision to change the mascot was approved by the board in May 1988. A Mascot Committee was formed to educate the school community about the reasons for the change and to determine the process for selecting a new mascot. Informal surveys conducted by *Quiver* staff at that time found that the student body was almost split equally between those in favor of the change and those opposed to it. The Mascot Committee solicited name suggestions for a new mascot from anyone in the Minnehaha community through the school's *Arrow* publication. From the suggestions received, the committee chose three names and submitted them for a vote by K-12 students. The three names voted on in the spring of 1989 were the Panthers, receiving 46 percent of the vote; the Wolf Pack, receiving 36 percent of the vote; and the Express, receiving 18 percent of the vote. President Nelson took the name "Panthers" to the school board, which accepted it; however, concerns were raised at a faculty meeting regarding the decision and a vote was made to send the name back to the Mascot Committee. Because the Indian logo was already removed from some team uniforms in anticipation of the new mascot, further concerns were raised that the school would be mascot-less while the selection process continued.

A new Mascot Committee was formed in November 1989. Names were again solicited from the school community, resulting in a ballot of thirty-three mascot options. The list underwent a series of votes throughout the school year by students in grades six through twelve, the faculty, staff, and administration, reducing the selection to two potential mascots: the Redhawks and the Mavericks. After a vote in February 1990, Redhawks was chosen by the school community, and on March 13, 1990, the Redhawks mascot was approved by the Board of Education, officially becoming the new mascot of Minnehaha Academy.

MASCOT NAMES

1. Bengals
2. Black Hawks
3. Buckskins
4. Cardinals
5. Challengers
6. Cousers
7. Crimson Tide
8. Eagles
9. Explorers
10. Falcons
11. Flames
12. Guardians
13. Hawks
14. Lions
15. Matadors
16. Mavericks
17. Meteorites
18. Minutemen
19. Normans
20. Panthers
21. Pioneers
22. Red Eagles
23. Red Hawks
24. Red Tide
25. Red Wave
26. Rockets
27. Silver Bullets
28. Spiders
29. Trackers
30. Voyaguers
31. Wolfpack
32. Wolverines
33. Wolves

1980–1989 95

1990–1999

(Photos courtesy of Jim Nash)

96 MINNEHAHA ACADEMY: A CENTURY OF FAITH AND LEARNING

ENROLLMENT continued to drop in the early and mid-1990s, resulting in the smallest North Campus student body in forty years. The decrease resulted in fewer teachers, smaller classes, and less crowded halls. In 1990, the Academy changed its mascot from the Indians to the Redhawks. Despite the contraction, the school continued to expand its programming. A preschool was added at the South Campus in 1995, making the school an official PreK-12 institution. Bloomington Campus became Minnehaha Academy's first satellite campus in 1996. Craig Nelson retired from Minnehaha Academy in 1994 and went on to work as an educational consultant. Dr. John Engstrom became the seventh president of the Academy in 1994. The school board made the conscious decision to select for the first time a president who was a professional educator rather than a member of the Covenant clergy. Among other accomplishments, Engstrom greatly expanded the school's Advanced Placement course offerings.

(Photo from the MA archives)

Dr. John B. Engstrom became the seventh president of Minnehaha Academy in 1994. Engstrom graduated from Wheaton College with a Bachelor of Science in Chemistry. He went on to the State University of New York at Stony Brook, where he obtained a Master of Arts in Liberal Studies and a Master of Science in Chemistry. In 1989, he completed a Ph.D. in Education in Science Education from Columbia University in New York City. At Minnehaha Academy, Engstrom increased the Advanced Placement courses offered and taught Advanced Placement Physics. He oversaw the opening of Minnehaha Academy's Bloomington Campus. He also led the campaign for the school's most recent building expansions.

(Photo from the MA archives)

Nancy Johnson came to MA in 1996 and taught economics and psychology until assuming the role of upper school principal in 2005.

(Photo from the MA archives)

Ann Sorenson taught upper school theater and film from 1993 to 2006. Under her direction, students wrote, directed, performed, and produced the film *How We Got Here* in 1999. The film was screened in the Riverview Theater and received media attention as the first such effort in the state of Minnesota. She also organized an annual Student Showcase with art teacher Becky Anderson to highlight the talents of students involved in art and drama.

(Photo from the MA archives)

Scott Scholl is an upper school math teacher who started at the Academy in 1994.

(Photo from the MA archives)

Ronald (Ron) Monson started as an upper school science teacher and middle school football coach in 1990. He is currently the director of athletic advancement.

98 MINNEHAHA ACADEMY: A CENTURY OF FAITH AND LEARNING

(Photo from the MA archives)

Mike DiNardo is the current upper school vice principal. He started teaching at the Academy in 1994 and has taught Foundations of Chemistry and Physics, AP Chemistry, AP Physics, Algebra I, and AP Statistics.

(Photo from the MA archives)

Greg Bestland is the South Campus chaplain and a Bible teacher. He leads the lower and middle school chapel services each week and started in 1999.

(Photo from the MA archives)

Ronette (Ronnie) George is a middle school art teacher who started at the Academy in 1996.

(Photo from the MA archives)

Jeffrey (Jeff) Crafton is an upper school sacred studies teacher and chapel coordinator who started at the Academy in 1996.

GORDON OLSON KNIGHTED

Choir director Gordon Olson retired after thirteen years at the Academy. Olson was knighted at his last Madrigal Dinner in 1999 in honor of his last year at the school. Olson established the Madrigal Singers and started the interdisciplinary production of the Madrigal Dinner when he first came to the school to take over the choral program from Harry Opel. He was also instrumental in organizing the school's Christmas concerts, spring musicals, and Singers' Tours.

(Photo from the MA archives)

A HI-TECH ACADEMY

The Academy greatly expanded its technology in the age of AOL and Netscape. In 1990, the school partnered with Lawrence Livermore Labs in California to offer students a class taught by Richard Enderton that used the lab's super computers. The school became one of the first in the U.S. involved in a national education super-computer program. In addition to installing a new computer lab, the school also installed a DIALOG Classmate Instruction Program, linking the school's computers to databases for research purposes. On November 16, 1996, the Academy was one of more than 150 schools in Minnesota that participated in "NetDay." NetDay was a national effort to wire school computers into the Internet, giving students and teachers access to the Internet's vast amount of educational resources. At Minnehaha's South Campus, five classrooms in the lower school were connected on NetDay, thanks to a dozen volunteers who diagrammed systems and pulled wires to hook up the classroom computers to the Internet. The upper school library also continued to receive significant technology donations including computers, printers, and educational CD-ROMs from Richard Hollinbeck, son of former librarian Frank Justus Hollinbeck.

Bonnie Morris, Ron Monson, and Merry Matson received an award in 1994 from the Pioneering Partners for Educational Technology project established by the Council of Great Lakes Governors. The award was given for the teachers' work on the school's sophomore interdisciplinary environmental project. The school was also awarded a grant for further technology integration (Nordstrom 2001, 94).

(Photo from the MA archives)

GREEN REDHAWKS

The Academy increased its environmental awareness with the founding of Y.E.S. (Young Earth Savers), an environmental club started by seven sophomores under the advisorship of Ron Monson. The club worked with the administration to advocate for expanded recycling efforts throughout the school, which also saved the school money in trash hauling. The school held its first Environmental Summit Conference on February 4, 1993. The conference was a daylong event for sophomores that featured panel presentations of research papers, speakers from conservation centers, and displays from local environmental businesses. Two seniors produced *Environews*, an environmental awareness newspaper, and the *Quiver* was printed on recycled paper. Currently, a student Earth Club continues to promote environmental awareness and lead activities such as Earth Day celebrations and walks around the school grounds to pick up trash, reminiscent of Campus Day many years before.

(Photo from the MA archives)

At the Environmental Summit, students also designed individual patches for a quilt, which were sewn together by Virginia Solvang. Bonnie Morris led the quilt project. The quilt currently hangs in the North Campus library.

A DIVERSE ACADEMY

The Academy actively sought to expand and support the economic and ethnic diversity of its student body at a time when students of color counted less than 10 percent of the high school enrollment. The Student Cultural Awareness Group was formed and organized an annual Festival of Nations. The festival featured student booths displaying food, clothing, and crafts from students' different ethnic heritages, as well as presentations by professional artists. Then it became known as the Culture Fair. The group was also responsible for organizing the first annual Black History Month Chapel. The Student Cultural Awareness group became True COLORS (Crossing Over Lines of Racial Stereotypes) in 2001 and is now known as the Student Diversity Club. Though the Culture Fair is no longer held, the club continues to be involved in service projects, chapel presentations, and discussions about diversity at the school. A focus on diversity included expansions of curriculum, such as the introduction of multicultural literature in the English Department. Warren Grantham was hired as the school's first diversity director in 1998 and became the advisor for the Students for Cultural Awareness. The school also drafted and approved a diversity policy in 1999.

The first annual MA Festival of Nations was held on October 19, 1994. The festival developed into a Culture Fair that expanded into a Culture Week and included the language programs in later years.

(Photo from the MA archives)

THE PERFECT SEASON

Both the boys' and girls' varsity soccer teams advanced to the state tournament in 1991. The girls' soccer team made appearances in the state tournament in 1990, 1991, and 1998. In 1998 the girls' varsity soccer team became the Tri-Metro Conference and Class AA State Champion with a record of 23-0-0. The team outscored opponents 80 to 2, and goalkeeper Gretchen Bratnober had twenty-two shutouts, earning her a place in the "Faces in the Crowd" section of *Sports Illustrated* magazine.

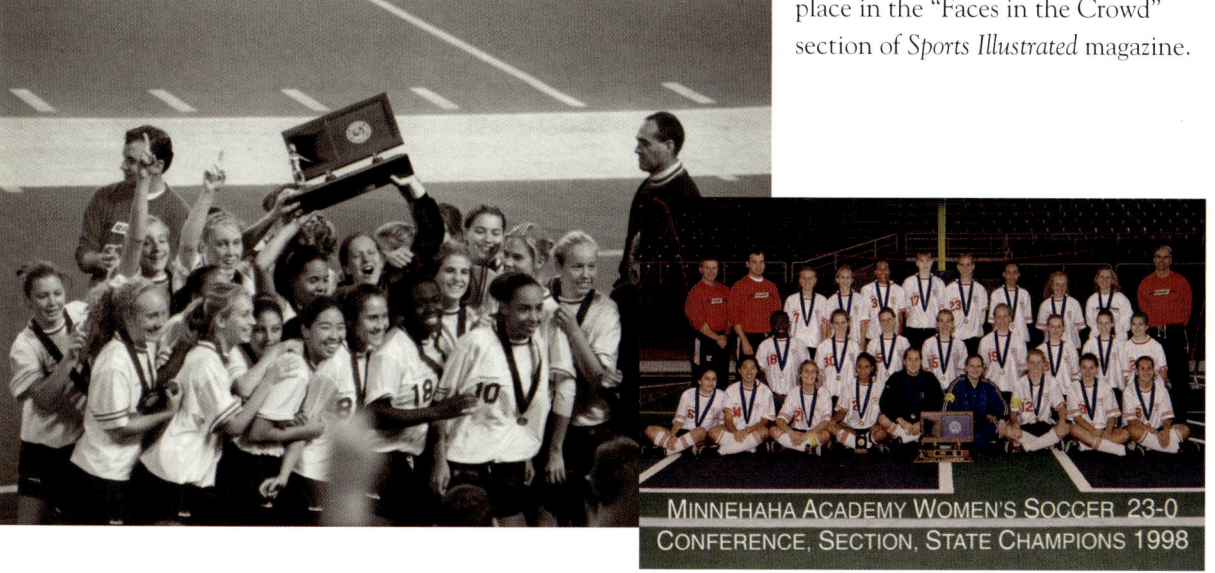

(Photos from the MA archives)

A FEW FIRSTS OF THE 1990s

- In 1998, the school graduated nine students from the Academy's first kindergarten class. These nine students were the first class to complete the full K-12 education at Minnehaha Academy.

- The school's spring performance of Shakespeare's *Much Ado About Nothing* in 1997 involved over sixty students, including thirty-six performers, and was the first time that Shakespeare had been performed at the school.

- In 1994, the Minnehaha Academy libraries were automated to give students electronic access to the card catalog.

- Girls' hockey started in 1994. Girls' swimming and diving joined with Blake to become the Bearhawks in 1995.

- The boys' basketball team went to the state tournament for the first time in Minnehaha history in 1996. The team ended the regular season 21-1 and went on to take fourth place in state.

(Photo from the MA archives)

AROUND CAMPUS

On September 7, 1996, Minnehaha Academy's soccer field was named Guido Kauls Field in recognition of teacher and soccer coach Guido Kauls' historic contributions to soccer both at Minnehaha Academy and in the state of Minnesota. In addition to starting the boys' and girls' soccer teams at MA, Kauls was named Minnesota Soccer Coach of the Year in 1981 and 1995 and Midwest Soccer Coach of the Year in 1982. He was nominated for National Coach of the Year in 1983. He became a charter member of the Minnesota Soccer Coaches Hall of Fame in 1991 and the MASL Hall of Fame in 1993.

(Photo from the MA archives)

Following the change of the school's mascot from the Indians to the Redhawks in 1990, the school newspaper also adopted a new identity. In 1992, the student newspaper changed its name to the *Talon*. The first *Talon* was published on October 2, 1992. The final issue of the *Quiver* was published on October 30, 1992.

(Images from the MA archives)

102   MINNEHAHA ACADEMY: A CENTURY OF FAITH AND LEARNING

IF THESE FLOORBOARDS
COULD SPEAK...

The Bloomington Campus operated for fifteen years, from 1996 to 2011, before being consolidated with the lower school of Minnehaha Academy's South Campus. At the time of its closing, students and parents gathered to celebrate the school and share their memories from its fifteen years in operation (excerpts from the *Arrow*, Summer 2011):

"The Monarch butterfly project with Mrs. Newhouse. I would call my grandmother in Florida every day to ask if she had seen my butterfly."

"Christmas caroling around the halls on the last day of school before Christmas. Parents walked in and the teachers and kids lined the sides of the halls and sang carols to them as they entered the building."

"The teachers and kids running laps around the halls in the morning (before school) for exercise."

(Photos from the MA archives)

"Going on a strike and marching around the gym to try to get more pizza at lunch."

"All the grades singing the songs together at the end-of-the-year celebration, and the principal announcing the 'new' fifth grade class, the 'new' fourth grade class, etc. This was a happy time, but when the kids were in fourth and fifth grade, it was a real tear-jerker because it was getting near the last time of being part of this wonderful school."

"Having the kids come home and tell me that they saw a dead body at school! (There was a funeral at the church.)"

"When the kids were in kindergarten, first and second grade, thinking that the kids over on the 'older' hallway (third-fifth grade hallway) were so old and so big!"

"For our family, this campus has been such an enormous blessing. For 11 years we've been driving to this campus to see our kids loved and nurtured and grow. They not only gained an amazing education, but they also learned how to be respectful and kind to kids of all ages, how to be a good example, a hard worker, fair, considerate, and how to be a good friend. We shared many joys and many sorrows as a school community that most people don't ever get to experience in a school setting. We were like a family. We have lifelong relationships that have come from this school and we are incredibly grateful for everything."

In 1995, Kathy Johnson, then lower school principal, was called into President John Engstrom's office and asked to start a suburban lower school. In the process of establishing Bloomington Campus, Kathy Johnson sought out teachers who would be willing to aid her in the tremendous task. South Campus teachers Kathy Fretheim and Mary Newhouse consented to dive into the new endeavor. The three women were integral to the opening of Bloomington Campus the following fall.

Bringing concepts to life for the youngest students has been the thrill and challenge of the Academy's middle and lower school teachers at the South Campus and Bloomington Campus. As the following sample of classroom projects illustrates, the Academy's faculty are experts at the task.

Fourth-grade teachers Kristen Tewinkel and Kathy Fretheim were known for their dynamic and creative geography projects, which included perhaps the most delicious geography lesson ever taught. Each student would be assigned a state to study. Culminating research, writing, and presenting on the state, students would then, with the help of parents, bake and shape a cake in the form of their chosen state. Students would bring all their cakes together, assembling an edible United States to be enjoyed by all.

(Photos from the MA archives)

Books, of course, are integral to education, but whereas high school students might dread the density of some of the textbooks they're required to read, middle and lower school programs are designed to promote the fun and imagination of reading. In addition to an annual Scholastic Book Fair, Book Weeks were held at the Bloomington and South campuses, which both concluded with a Book Character Parade in which students dressed as their favorite fictional characters and paraded through the schools.

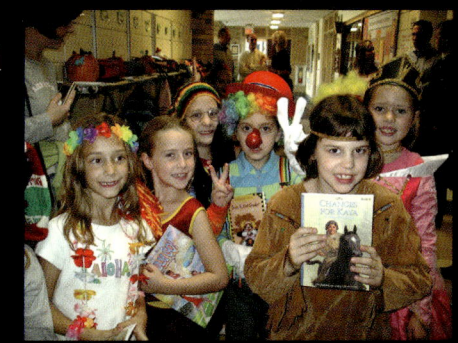

(Photo from the MA archives)

When President John Engstrom came in the 1990s he brought with him a love for all things science, and advocated for a lower school science project option. Begun at South Campus, but flourishing at Bloomington, lower school students have had the opportunity to do science experiments and produce the results of their work for informal judges who talk to them about what they have learned. In 2012, fourth-grade students were required to participate, but students from other grades were welcomed also. To generate enthusiasm for this parent-driven event, lower school teacher Blake Christianson created "Banana Man" complete with costume and postcard reminders.

(Photos from the MA archives)

104 MINNEHAHA ACADEMY: A CENTURY OF FAITH AND LEARNING

Encouraging a spirit of service in students is an important part of Minnehaha Academy's approach to Christian education. Serve It Day provides a service learning opportunity for middle school students in sixth, seventh, and eighth grades to become involved in the community. With the aid of parent volunteers, students have packed meals for Feed My Starving Children, spent time with residents of nursing homes, collected shoes for Soles to Souls, collected relief supplies for hurricane victims, and cleaned tombstones among a variety of other activities.

(Photos from the MA archives)

The Mississippi River has proven to be a rich resource for many different classes at the Academy because of its close proximity. The Seventh Grade River Project, started in 1996 when then middle school principal Dean Erickson asked his faculty to develop an interdisciplinary unit, asks students to explore an issue related to the river that students are interested in. After spending time researching, taking field trips along the river, and preparing presentations, a Convention Day is held when all the students present their issues.

(Photos from the MA archives)

Bob Noble, Bloomington Campus teacher from 1998 to 2011, led a Civil War re-enactment for fourth- and fifth-graders at both of the Academy's lower campuses as the culmination of a month-long study of the American Civil War. The project included a reenactment of Picket's Charge at the Battle of Gettysburg and a field hospital scene representing what it was like to be attended on the battlefield after the battle.

(Photos from the MA archives)

1990–1999 105

2000–2012

(Photos courtesy of Jim Nash)

106   Minnehaha Academy: A Century of Faith and Learning

Under President Engstrom, Minnehaha Academy launched the Promise for the Future Campaign in 2001 to renovate the North Campus and the Foundation for a Lifetime Campaign in 2007 to renovate the South Campus. Engstrom resigned in 2009 to become president at the Seoul Foreign School in Seoul, South Korea. Dr. Donna M. Harris received the call and moved from her home state of California to commence her tenure as Minnehaha Academy's eighth and current president, becoming the first woman of color to hold the position. The early 2000s saw a significant increase in enrollment, but this increase dropped following the 2009 recession. Due to the decreased enrollment, Bloomington Campus was consolidated with the Minneapolis Lower School at Minnehaha Academy's South Campus in 2011. Despite the contraction, the 2000s have ushered in a number of other landmarks. The school welcomed the third- and fourth-generation students of some families whose members first graduated from the Academy in 1916. Increasing diversity among the student body has included record numbers of students from other countries, including Canada, France, the Dominican Republic, Sudan, Ethiopia, Ecuador, Chad, Paraguay, Mexico, China, the Philippines, Peru, Switzerland, Argentina, Sweden, South Korea, Nigeria, Liberia, Latvia, and the Democratic Republic of the Congo. And, of course, the school celebrates its Centennial in 2013.

MEET THE NEW LEADERSHIP OF MINNEHAHA ACADEMY

(Photo from the MA archives)

Dr. Donna M. Harris is Minnehaha Academy's eighth and current president. After serving for two years as a missionary in South American prisons and churches, she received her bachelor's degree in 1987, a master's degree in education from San Jose State University in 2002, and her doctoral degree in education from the University of San Francisco in 2008. She has been a math teacher for eleven years, the director of curriculum and instruction at Valley Christian Schools for eight years, and the assistant superintendent and chief academic officer of Valley Christian Schools in the San Francisco Bay Area. She has also served as the children's pastor, worship leader, and elder at South Bay Community Church. Harris answered the call to the presidency of Minnehaha Academy, commencing her tenure on July 22, 2009. She was inaugurated on Sunday, September 13, 2009.

(Photo from the MA archives)

Barb Fjelstad is the director of curriculum. She started at the Academy in 2009.

(Photo from the MA archives)

Paulita Todhunter is the current director of diversity. She serves as the advisor for the upper school Diversity Club and the Student of Color Support Groups. She also teaches middle school math. Todhunter started at the Academy in 2000.

(Photo from the MA archives)

Homar Ramierez is the athletic director. He started at the Academy in January of 2012.

(Photo from the MA archives)

Bruce Maeda is the PreK-8 principal. He started at the Academy in 2010.

Bonnie Anderson is the director of human resources. She started at the Academy in 2001.

(Photo from the MA archives)

Janet Gulden is the South Campus vice principal. She started at the Academy in 2010.

(Photo from the MA archives)

108 MINNEHAHA ACADEMY: A CENTURY OF FAITH AND LEARNING

(Photo from the MA archives)

Sara Stone is the executive director of institutional advancement. She started at the Academy in 2012.

(Photo from the MA archives)

Lauren Bae is an upper school counselor. She started at the Academy in 2011.

(Photo from the MA archives)

Richard Harris is the upper school college and guidance counselor. He started at the Academy in 2010.

GUIDO KAULS HONORED

After retiring in the spring of 2001, Guido Kauls received a Career Award for Outstanding Teaching of German from the Minnesota Association of Teachers of German in October 2001. On November 10, 2001, Kauls was inducted into the Minnesota State High School Coaches Association—the first soccer coach to receive the honor. In March 2002, he was inducted into the Minnesota State High School League Hall of Fame. He was also voted boys' soccer National Coach of the Year 2001 by the National Federation Coaches Association, becoming the first soccer coach from Minnesota and the second Minnesota coach from any sport to win the award.

(Photo from the MA archives)

A DREAM FULFILLED

On May 17, 2003, middle school band instructor Paul Isaacs had the opportunity to conduct the Saint Paul Chamber Orchestra in a performance of Grieg's *In the Hall of the Mountain King*. Isaacs was gifted the opportunity by an MA parent who purchased the chance to conduct at an SPCO gala event. Isaacs recalled, "During the concert Mr. [Andreas] Delfs [the SPCO conductor] introduced me to the audience, and it was explained that the people who usually purchase this opportunity usually cannot conduct, and that the orchestra then plays 'the Stars and Stripes' which is 'conductor proof.' It was further explained that a parent had purchased this as a gift to his children's band teacher, and that since I could conduct, they had given me a piece that required a conductor. [...] Conducting a world class orchestra fulfilled a dream that I had had since I was about six. It was truly the experience of a lifetime" (*Arrow*, Summer 2003).

(Photo from the MA archives)

2000–2012 109

(Photo from the MA archives)

A NEW MA FOR A NEW MILLENNIUM

The upper school fully converted to block scheduling in the early 2000s. Block scheduling meant that Mondays were reserved for the traditional seven forty-minute periods in a day, while Tuesday-through-Friday classes were extended to eighty minutes and the seven classes were divided between odd periods held on Wednesday and Friday and even periods held on Tuesday and Thursday. New school advisor groups, different from those in the past, were now gender-specific. The idea behind the gender separation was to encourage everyone to be more open and participate in discussions. To help strengthen the relationships, students stay with the same group all through their high school careers. Curriculum changes included the addition of Mandarin Chinese to the school's world language program. The Introduction to Business class, hearkening back to the early days of business courses at the Academy, now teaches personal finance, interview and job skills, résumé and cover letter writing, and investing. The school offered AP World History for the first time in 2005 and currently offers seventeen AP courses total. In 2004, the school provided 17 percent of its students with financial assistance, remaining committed to extending the Minnehaha experience to all of its students, regardless of financial need.

NEW TRADITIONS

The Academy held its first annual Scandinavian Holiday Festival in 2007. The event featured a Christmas dinner, entertainment, and a holiday market of local arts and crafts. Proceeds went to the support of Minnehaha's Annual Fund. The festival replaced the Minnehaha Holiday House Tour.

The Student Intern Program was started at the Academy in 2002. Students have to apply and be accepted into the program, after which they receive training during leadership retreats over the summer. Interns serve in a variety of roles throughout the school. Service interns oversee the organization of school-wide service projects, publicity interns provide public announcements, assembly and chapel interns help plan and coordinate chapel services and assembly programs, and social interns and athletic interns assist in the planning of school dances and athletic events. In 2007, the Student Intern Program replaced the Student Council.

(Photo from the MA archives)

(Photo from the MA archives)

MINNEHAHA ACADEMY: A CENTURY OF FAITH AND LEARNING

NEW WORSHIP

The Spiritual Life Committee strove to make chapels more appealing to the students by creating a "camp" atmosphere, including more contemporary songs and themes relevant to the worship music, and singing led by the newly created Praise Band. Sonlight, a prayer and sharing group started in the 1990s, moved to the Singers' room due to large attendance and split into three sections: Sonlight Bible study and worship band, Prayer Warriors held every Tuesday and Thursday morning from 8 to 8:30 a.m. for prayer and Bible study, and Louder Than Words, a group that went out once a month to perform community service. MILK (Music in Light of the King) was a monthly worship held in the Hognander Chapel. The program was not a requirement of the school and attracted students from outside the school, such as from Minneapolis South High. In addition to chapel, middle school students participated in Bible classes, service hours, and a two-year journal project called "The Bible Study Notebook." They helped with food shelves, baby-sitting, raking leaves, and visiting nursing homes, taking a serious look at the word of God and how it applies to their lives.

NEW TEAMS

The Academy added another state champion team to its roster in 2010 when the girls' basketball team won the Class AA State Championship for the first time in the school's history. In 2009, the girls' softball team became the Tri-Metro Conference Champion and went on to place second in the state tournament.

Girls' lacrosse began its first season as an official MSHSL sport at the Academy in 2003.

The Academy currently offers twenty-seven varsity sports at the upper school. Fluctuating enrollment and varied student interest means that some of the school's teams operate as co-ops with one or more schools, including the girls' hockey team known as the Saints, the girls' swimming team known as Metro United, and the boys' wrestling team known for many years as the Knighthawks.

(Photo courtesy of Jim Nash)

(Photo from the MA archives)

(Photo courtesy of Reid Westrem)

2000–2012 111

NEW FIRSTS FOR THE **NEW MILLENIUM**

- The first play performed in the North Campus' new Fine Arts Center in 2003 was Eugene O'Neil's *Ah, Wilderness*.

- The school hosted its first Annual Alumni Career Day in 2009, inviting alumni back to talk with students and answer questions about their careers.

- On April 22–24, 2004, the school hosted the Northwest Conference's annual meeting for the first time in its new facilities. Minnehaha Academy will again host the annual meeting in 2013 as part of the school's Centennial celebration.

- The new Athletic Center allowed the school to host its first wrestling tournament, the Knighthawk Wrestling Classic invitational, on January 18, 2003. The tournament featured nine Minnesota teams competing in the one-day event. The Academy's wrestling team was then a cooperative with Minneapolis Lutheran High School. The tournament has been held for the past ten years.

(Photo from the MA archives)

AROUND CAMPUS

In 2001, Gerald Nordstrom wrote and published *Where Youth Meets Truth: A History of Minnehaha Academy*. Nordstrom taught English, studio art, art, and church history at the Academy's upper school from 1959 to 1993. He also served as the director of more than fifty school plays and musicals over a period of twenty years. Copies of the book are currently available.

In 2001, the school's first debate team in twenty-three years made its appearance with the slogan "A Tradition Reborn," acknowledging the Academy's long and decorated debate program. The new team joined fifty-nine other first-year teams from twelve schools in their first tournament at St. Paul Academy, placing first overall and being the only school with two undefeated teams. The Minnehaha Debate Team currently participates in the Classic Debate League, which includes strong teams from many of the Metro area's biggest schools.

(Image from the MA archives)

(Photo from the MA archives)

112   Minnehaha Academy: A Century of Faith and Learning

IF THESE FLOORBOARDS
COULD SPEAK...

"TYPICALLY, OUR CONVERSATIONS would begin by Paul saying, 'I've got one for you,' and our time together would start off with a joke, followed by a laugh—or a groan. In more than a quarter century of close friendship and collaboration, I came to know Paul Isaacs, not just as a man of humor, but as a man of remarkable talent and personality.

"Paul Isaacs was a musician of highest caliber. His compositions, arrangements, and performances were always spot on, be it a concert, wedding, CD, or a silly skit or song—of which there were many.

"Paul Isaacs was one of the best teachers I have ever known. Consider the skill needed to invite 50-60 Middle School students into your room, give them all noisemakers, and then in a few short months have them perform beautiful music. And beautiful music it was.

"Paul Isaacs was always ready to laugh—and make others laugh. Those who knew Paul as student, colleague, or friend know exactly what I'm talking about.

"Paul Isaacs had a huge heart for God and for those around him. He had an enormous impact on countless students through the years, as they experienced his sincere concern for them as individuals. The life lessons he passed on to so many students (and friends and colleagues) may just be his greatest legacy.

"It's terribly difficult to lose a close friend. But I also celebrate a life extremely well lived in the promise of the Resurrection, and I count myself blessed to have had my life intersect with his. And when it is my turn to walk through the pearly gates, I expect that one of the first things I will hear will be a familiar voice saying, 'Hey, Rich, I've got one for you.'"

Rich Enderton, upper school math teacher
(*Arrow*, Summer 2010)

"What I really appreciate about Ms. Fondell is that she taught history not with an emphasis on dates and facts, but with an emphasis on the real people who lived their lives and shaped our world in important ways. That philosophy was so apparent in how she treated her students: not as pupils who needed to get through material and complete curricular standards, but as people whom she believed could have a big impact on our world. One of my favorite middle school memories was the last day of U.S. History class when Ms. Fondell dimmed the lights and played Bob Dylan's 'Forever Young.' I could tell that she truly wished those lyrics for each one of the students she has ever taught."

Tim Dwight '05
(*Arrow*, Fall 2011)

"Ms. Fondell was my middle school teacher. My friends and I loved her. Sometimes we would skip lunch to hang out with Ms. Fondell and she made us feel important and cared about. I have thought about her many times over the past few years as I now teach middle school as well. There are times when kids want to talk after school or hang out during lunch and even if I'm not in the mood, I think about Ms. Fondell and how much it meant to us when she gave us her attention and time. So what I learned from Ms. Fondell is being passed to other kids."

Rebecca Brower '94
(*Arrow*, Fall 2011)

FAREWELL FROM MINNEHAHA ACADEMY

In the natural rhythm of a school, the end of every year wishes farewell to another graduating class. Nearly 12,000 students have passed through Baccalaureate and Commencement ceremonies, joining the ranks of Minnehaha Academy alumni.

Early Commencement and Baccalaureate ceremonies were held at local Covenant churches, most notably the Swedish Tabernacles, now known as First Covenant Church in Minneapolis (pictured right) and First Covenant Church in St. Paul (pictured above).

(Photos from the MA archives)

114 MINNEHAHA ACADEMY: A CENTURY OF FAITH AND LEARNING

(Photos from the MA archives)

When the space has been available, the school has held Commencement and Baccalaureate ceremonies on campus.

Beginning in the 1990s and continuing to the present, Commencement is currently held at Benson Great Hall on the campus of Bethel University. After the 2000s remodeling and continuing to the present, Baccalaureate is held in the North Campus Hognander Chapel.

2000–2012 115

Future Legacy: 2013–
Another Hundred Years

Minnehaha Academy has changed in remarkable ways over a century of experience. Through all its changes, the school's two core values of academic excellence and Christian faith have remained consistent, but many predictions about what the school might look like in the future have also been made. Such predictions have been made by members of the school community in all capacities, including students, faculty, and administrators. Some of these predictions have been realized while others remain unfulfilled. The following are just a few highlights of these visions for MA's future imagined by past generations.

The 1931 *Antler* contains a fictional piece titled "'31—The Untrodden Path of the Future—'61" in which two girls discuss imagined life at Minnehaha Academy in 1961. Their imaginings include reference to an Alumni Hotel with a Publication Room that keeps all the old *Quivers*, *Quills*, and *Antlers* on file and an addition of a grade school and a kindergarten to the Academy. The grade school and kindergarten were realized in the 1980s and 1990s. The Minnehaha Alumni/Archive House was established in late 2011 in preparation for the school's Centennial celebration. The house is located at 3105 46th Avenue S, Minneapolis, at the northwest corner of the North Campus soccer field and directly behind the Northwest Conference offices. All are invited to visit the house, peruse old school materials, share stories, and relive memories.

116   Minnehaha Academy: A Century of Faith and Learning

The school community wrestled with the issue of establishing dormitory facilities from the earliest decades well into the 1950s. A Girls' Dormitory Fund was started in 1929. The school continued to receive money for this fund from individuals and groups specifically interested in building a girls' dormitory in the 1930s, but the conditions of the school weren't suitable for building at that time. In 1951, however, the issue came up again according to the minutes from a Board of Education meeting: "The home on the River Road is still available to us. Further reports indicate that the neighbors in the immediate vicinity of the residence are favorable to its use as a girls' dormitory. Serious deliberation should be made of this project since it appears to be an opportunity which may not come again for some time. If action could be taken in the next few weeks our appeal to the northwest constituency outside of the Twin Cities would be greatly enhanced." In 1955, the board continued to deliberate the question, "What should be the extent of our field of service?" about which they commented, "The question was raised as to whether we should expect people outside of the Twin Cities to support the school when we have no dormitory facilities to offer so that their children can attend the school. Should we try to broaden our field of service by making more adequate provision for out-of-town students or should we frankly admit that we are a Twin Cities school? The president and business manager of the school stated that there are a number of out-of-town people each year who inquire about whether or not the school has dormitory accommodations, and who would send their children if they felt they would be adequately housed and supervised." Ultimately, no dormitory facilities were ever built, but it's worth noting how long the school addressed the issue as it related to the Academy's identity and influence in the surrounding communities and as part of the Northwest Conference of the Covenant Church.

The class of 1936 produced a scrapbook for president Theodore W. Anderson in which they included essay selections titled, "Minnehaha Academy as I Should Like to See It in the Future." Many of the essays expressed wishes to see the school continue to grow as a Christian institution. One of the more specific suggestions made in several of the essays was that an indoor connection be provided between the 1913 and 1922 buildings. The Northwest-Minnehaha Advance Campaign of 1946–1949 provided this connection. Prior to the campaign, students had to travel outdoors from one building to the other and a canvassed "hall" was created to provide some limited protection from the Minnesota winters (as seen in the photo of the school building at left).

In the 1988 *Antler*, one student made the suggestion that the school should build a three-level heated parking ramp. While no such ramp has yet been built, the expansions of the school over the years have greatly improved and developed the parking lots for students and faculty.

Following the opening of the Bloomington Campus in 1996, President John Engstrom mentioned the possibility of expansion to other locations, which included the idea of starting an Urban Early Childhood Center as well as establishing other satellite campuses. The Summer 2000 *Arrow* included notice of a Minnehaha Academy Maple Grove Campus set to open in the fall of 2001, which, despite the announcement, never became a reality.

During the South Campus renovations in 2006 and 2007, the South Campus community was asked in a survey, "What Would the Students Like Built?" Kindergarten through eighth grade responses included suggestions for a kids' lounge, mini refrigerators by each kid's desk, a swimming pool, a theater, and an ice cream shop. One of the teachers expressed the desire for "chairs that don't squeak in chapel and a bathroom just for teachers."

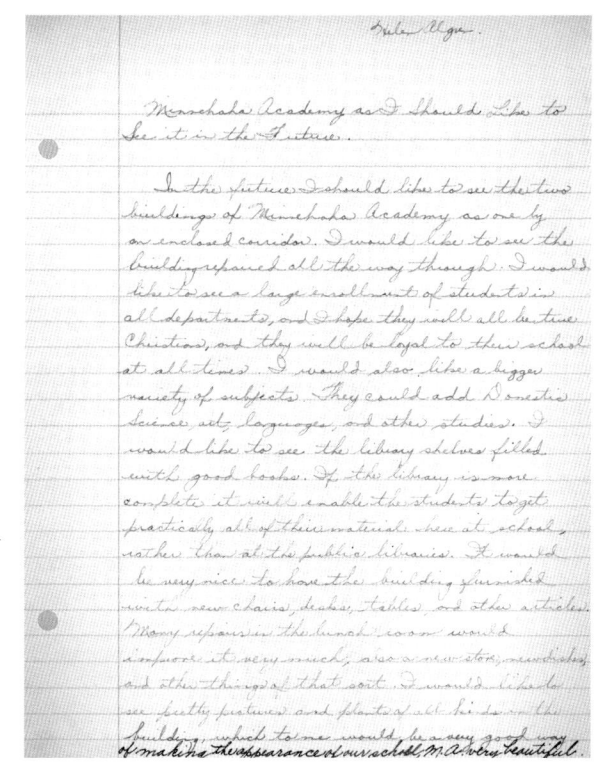

118   MINNEHAHA ACADEMY: A CENTURY OF FAITH AND LEARNING

MINNEHAHA ACADEMY AS YOU SHOULD LIKE TO SEE IT IN THE FUTURE

Will students one day be riding to school in flying cars? Will Minnehaha Academy open a true "satellite" campus on the moon? Collected here are a few predictions of what the Academy might look like in another hundred years, courtesy of thoughtful students from Reid Westram's 2011 Intermediate and Advanced Journalism classes.

"Instead of books and notebooks, every student will have a screen; today's interactive classroom whiteboards ('SmartBoard' or 'Promethean Board') will develop and become personalized, and each student will have one."

"Lunches will be offered in buffet style, with various stations offering different types of food."

"Biology students will dissect virtual, three-dimensional cats. History students will be able to 'walk through' a virtual Pompeii (as videogame technology develops, educational applications will follow)."

"Debates will continue over whether American students work too hard or too little in school; either way, each student's class load will be smaller (fewer courses per semester)."

"Some thought that the average Minnehaha graduate will be expected to earn a master's degree at minimum; others thought the opposite would happen, with rising college tuition and shifting employment, more and more M.A. graduates will learn specific trades and skip the traditional four-year college route."

"High-school courses will address everyday life skills issues (personal finance, relationships) as well as academic issues, as societal problems reveal an increasing need for those skills."

"There will be more language-immersion options at earlier (elementary) grades, as Americans have an increasing need to be multilingual."

"In competition, more academic games will return to prominence (e.g., chess)… not just athletics."

"Students will specialize earlier in their academic careers. Today, students declare a 'major' in college, but in the future there will be the equivalent sort of majors in high school."

"Driverless cars….? Grades won't exist….?"

WORDS OF THE PAST FOR THE FUTURE

Leaders of Minnehaha Academy have often looked to the past when considering the school's future. Here are a few words from the presidents that reflect what the history of the school offers for the generations to come.

THEODORE W. ANDERSON, 1913–1933

"From the land of the midnight sun, signally blessed of God also in spiritual light, came our Covenant trail blazers a few decades ago. They were young, enterprising, and undaunted by the hardships of the frontier inevitably faced in the land of their adoption. Their achievements on American soil constitute an epic. Into the life of their promised land they poured their wealth of devotion and purposeful toil. Pioneers of a new day of religious freedom and economic liberty they not only felled the forest and broke the prairie, but also by unstinting sacrifice and resolute perseverance, built churches, Christian schools, and institutions of mercy.

"Heirs of a rich and hallowed past we face the challenge of making a similar impact on our own generation in a day of confusion and dire need. We honor our predecessors most worthily by perpetuating and enlarging this sacred heritage.

"Let us go forward courageously as torch-bearers for Christ and His Church." ("A Tribute to the Founders and Pioneer Builders of The Mission Covenant Church of America," presented under the auspices of the Saint Paul Covenant Woman's Auxiliary, Minnehaha Academy, December 8, 1939)

EMANUEL O. FRANKLIN, 1938–1943

"The panorama of progress of Minnehaha Academy, from its first year down to the present, cannot but give much cause for admiration, optimism, faith and gratitude. The increase in material equipment and educational facilities, the enrichment of the curriculum, the broadening of service to an ever-increasing student body, and the widening circle of alumni and friends—all testify to the dynamic power of the sacrificial devotion of her educational staffs, past and present; to the healthy, happy school-family spirit; and, above all, to the multiple blessing and continual guidance of God.

"Looking back, we can all remember some valleys of depression and hardship and some elevations of joy and success. Nothing of value is gained without sweat and tears. But the sweat need not be, and is not, always the groping labor of the shadows; or the tears, the tears of disappointment and failure. More than these, have been the labors of triumph and tears of joy—or Minnehaha Academy would not be what it is today." (*Forty Years in Faith*, 5)

CLARENCE A. NELSON, 1943–1949

"It has been my good fortune to see Minnehaha from two vantage points. In its early days, when its saga was just beginning to unfold, and its educational activity was confined to Old Main, I knew it as its students knew it. Even now the soft fragrance of its small beginnings fills my soul with nostalgia, that comes from another world. How calm and artless life seemed then. With ease and satisfaction I recall my teachers and school mates: images that time has not touched, voices as distinct as in those happy hours. Three years and four months I shared that carefree life, and often in after-years I have thanked God for the plain goodness of it all.

"Twenty-five years later I was back at 'the fairest jewel' on Mississippi's banks. This was only meant to be a part-time assignment, added to the full-time pastoral ministry, until a new president could be secured. But, as so often happens, the casual task became an overpowering master and almost before we realized it Minnehaha and I had worked together six years and three months. I saw in the old school a courage and determination that I did not know she carried under her tender love for youth. What an adventure. What friendships! Again kind faces and familiar voices beguile me. What treasures they have hid in the soul; richer than gold or gems. They pass in review,—the Singers tours into Northern Minnesota during the Advance,—the students' Advance campaign, netting $22,000,—the Chapel memorial service in honor of our martyred China-missionary, Martha Anderson,—the decision to build into brick and mortar the dreams of years,—the sudden homegoing of our incomparable Prof. Pearson,—the dedication of new edifices, which meant my task was accomplished,—and then the painful and almost unnoticed departure to other duties. These are the precious, deeply-colored threads that weave themselves into the lovely pattern which means only one thing to my life,—Minnehaha Academy." (*Forty Years in Faith*, 6)

ARTHUR W. ANDERSON, 1950–1959

"Try as you might, it is impossible to go back and satisfactorily recover the experiences of the past. When the average alumnus returns he is bewildered about the physical changes that have taken place.

"How do we get to the gym?

"Where is the main office?

"Where is Chapel located and how do we get there?

"These are the questions we are frequently called upon to answer. Rekindled memories move upon us like a nostalgia but we cannot return to the experiences which prompt them.

"What then? One cannot be equally sincere in saying that one who has been at Minnehaha Academy never leaves it. Conditions change, to be sure, as they ought to. But we all belong to this continuing ministry—dreaming its dreams, sharing its fellowship, caring in its concerns." (*The Alumnus*, March 1952)

WILBUR M. WESTERDAHL, 1960–1976

"Despite widespread rumors to the contrary, the classroom teacher is here to stay. Like Mark Twain's response to the rumor of his death, reports of the imminent disappearance of the classroom teacher from the educational scene have been grossly exaggerated. The role of the teacher is changing, to be sure, but he will always remain at the heart of the learning process.

"The complexity of our modern world and the sheer weight of the numbers of human beings to be educated have prompted many to believe that the teacher's role is a diminishing one. Some phases of a teacher's work will diminish in emphasis and some phases may be replaced, but his over-all importance will actually be increased.

"The continuing temptation in education is to forget its beginnings and to emulate modern business and industry in efficiency and speed. Education in its origin was a small community of students and respected scholars in face-to-face relationships. This was and still must be the heart of learning." (*Arrow*, May 1968)

CRAIG W. NELSON, 1977–1994

"A few weeks ago now I attended a memorial service. The service remembered the life of the Rev. A. Milton Freedholm. Rev. Freedholm served the Bethlehem Covenant Church for 40 years as pastor. During that time, he was Dean of the Bible Institute at Minnehaha Academy. His service to the Covenant, Minnehaha and Bethlehem was long and faithful. As I listened to those who participated in the service, eulogizing Pastor Freedholm, I was particularly impressed by the emphasis given to his long ministry. According to the late Dr. Theodore W. Anderson, Pastor Freedholm's forty years at Bethlehem were the longest pastorate in the history of the Covenant church. Now, lest you misunderstand, the strength of this ministry resided not only in its length but also in its quality and faithfulness.

"I am impressed by this fact; probably because it stands out in such stark contrast to today's attitudes. Short-term goals, quick fixes, and the insistence on the immediate are all too common ingredients of life. Commitment is of little importance.

"[…] How strange and refreshing long-term commitment to a task, purpose, or people is.

"Such faithfulness demands something special. It demands that one see long-term effects. You cannot commit yourself to the quick cure or immediate goal and remain faithful over the long pull.

"Such faithfulness requires 'thick skin.' In any effort there are going to be problems, criticism and opposition. If one is going to persevere, one cannot be easily damaged by the slings and arrows of opposition. […]

"Finally, faithfulness requires a commitment to and dependence upon that which transcends us and our own experience. All too often in life we reach the end of our own resources. When this happens we are tempted to quit. The job grows tedious; people become boring; and that which was exciting becomes commonplace. When that happens, it is commitment to One greater than we are that sees us through. Here, I believe, was the secret of Milton Freedholm's life. He was committed to his Lord and Master, Jesus Christ, and thus able to be faithful over the long pull. So may it be with you and me as life unfolds before us and we are tempted to settle for the short-term goal." (*Arrow*, November 1986)

JOHN B. ENGSTROM, 1994–2009

"'Heritage: What is handed down from one generation to the next; an inheritance.'

"Among my greatest privileges is the opportunity to visit with alumni of Minnehaha Academy. […]

"During these times, I frequently ask our alumni to share memories of their days at Minnehaha. They tell hilarious stories of people playing tricks on their classmates and teachers, a stolen first kiss in the hallway, glorious accounts of victory on the field or the basketball court, and occasional long walks to the principal's office after a foiled prank.

"But after these funny stories, I hear accounts of an inheritance our alumni have taken with them throughout life. […]

"To hear these pieces of our school heritage is both encouraging and challenging. It is encouraging to learn of the incredible impact our Minnehaha graduates have had around the world for 85 years. At the same time, it is incredibly challenging to recognize the opportunity for eternal impact we have at Minnehaha, and for which we are held accountable.

"Our students are being handed an inheritance as they walk the halls, spend time in chapel, and interact with our faculty and staff in classes. I am thankful to say that our students today, just as they have for 85 years, are receiving a goodly inheritance through the foundation set by our alumni and past leaders. Our students can say along with the psalmist, 'Lord, you have assigned my portion in my cup; you have made my lot secure. The boundary lines have fallen for me in pleasant places; surely I have a delightful inheritance'" (Psalm 16:5). (*Arrow*, Fall 1998)

DONNA M. HARRIS, 2009–

"With God's help, Minnehaha Academy has left an indelible mark on the world. The school has been blessed with wise and effective leadership, talented faculty and staff, and lasting student contributions in ministry, music, art and athletics. With each new generation of students, the institution has remained vibrant and relevant, meeting the needs of diverse learners.

"Now, in the 21st Century, schools are poised to break out of the traditional paradigms of scheduling, educational delivery, and models of teaching. Teachers utilize emerging technologies such as mobile computing devices and personalized and interactive learning tools that allow for instructional flexibility, enhanced access to subject-matter experts, and global interaction and collaboration. At Minnehaha, it will be important to be sharply attuned to the education horizon to maintain our position in the marketplace, but even more critical, we must remember our God-inspired mission, lest we drift from it.

"The integration of Christian faith in learning must continue to be our heart's desire. We must remember that spiritual formation and developing the intellect are not mutually exclusive, so we must be faithful in both. We must remember the supremacy of the Bible, the Holy Scripture, the Old and the New Testament, as the Word of God and the only perfect rule for faith, doctrine, and conduct.

"We must remember that spiritual formation and the development of an authentic faith translates into students' engagement with the world. As leaders our love for God must be as fervent as when we first surrendered to Him and that love must overflow into our work and mission at Minnehaha. For the sake of future generations, we must commit to being God's sustainable resource." (Written by Donna Harris, 2012)

One Hundred Years at MA

A SCHOOL IS NOTHING without its students. Enrollment numbers can hardly be said to tell the whole story of Minnehaha Academy, but they do provide a broad picture of the school's history from the standpoint of how student numbers have been affected over the decades. The MA archives contain several simple enrollment graphs produced at various points in the school's history. Provided is the most current representation of enrollment figures over the past one hundred years (excluding enrollment for the 2012–2013 school year, which was not determined at the time of this book's publication). The following graph depicts total enrollment for Minnehaha Academy (the high school, middle school, lower school, and Bloomington Campus figures are all combined).

Total Student Enrollment

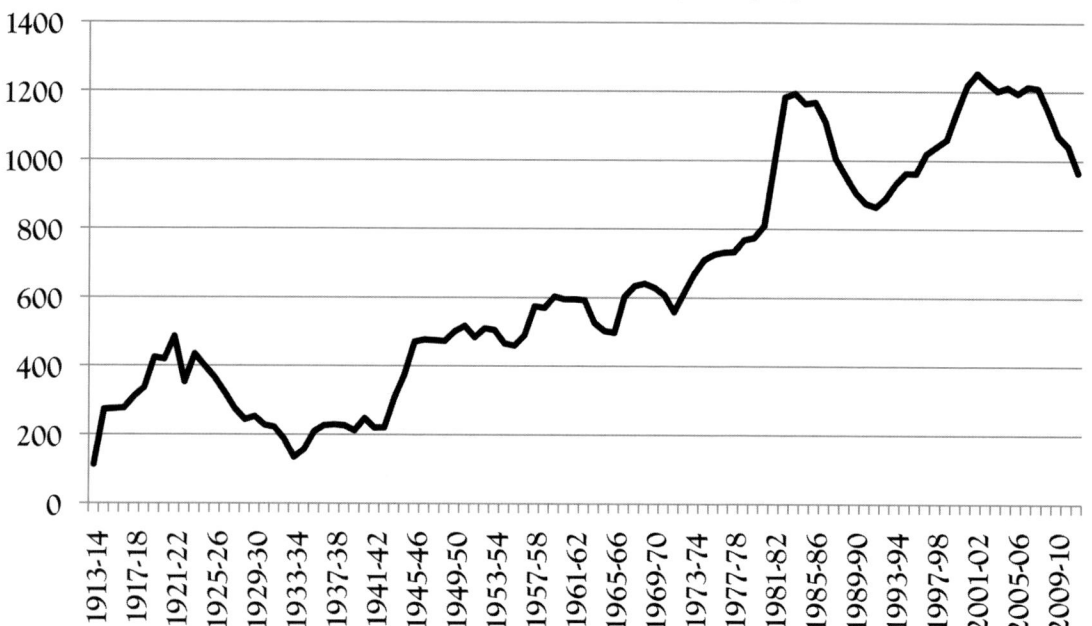

Faculty and Administration Years of Service

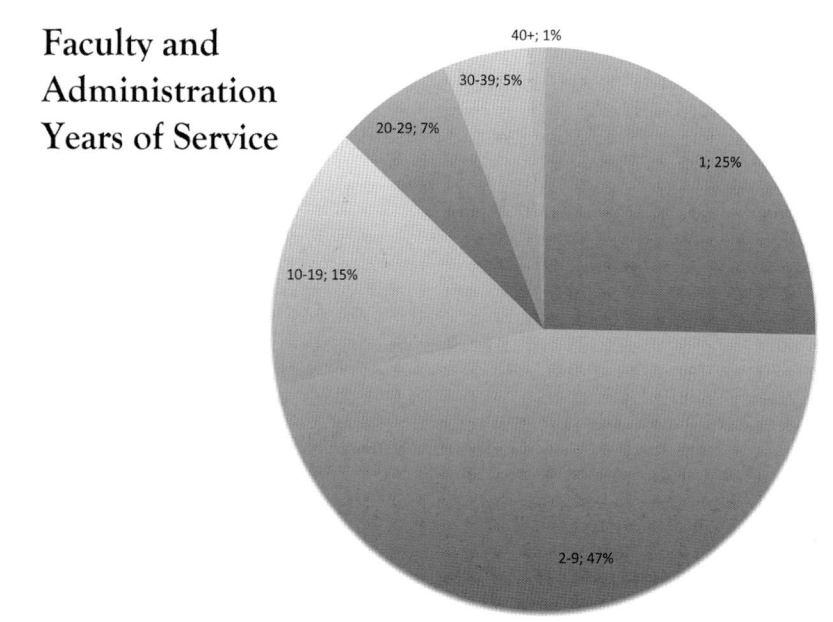

- 40+; 1%
- 30-39; 5%
- 20-29; 7%
- 10-19; 15%
- 2-9; 47%
- 1; 25%

A total of 584 faculty and administrators have served at the Academy. Of that total, 140 (25 percent) have taught for only one year and 161 (28 percent) have taught for ten or more years. The following chart illustrates the breakdown of length of service among teachers.

(Compiled from information gathered from the school's business office and other documents)

It is impossible to adequately honor all the administrators, teachers, and staff who have contributed to the success of Minnehaha Academy over one hundred years in such a brief space. Attempts have been made to highlight some of the people in each decade who have impacted the school by holding leadership positions, starting major programs, and serving for extended lengths of time, but truly every one has contributed an important part to making the school what it is today. Listed are the names of the eighty-nine faculty, administrators, and staff (15 percent) who have been at the Academy for twenty or more years.

20–29 YEARS OF SERVICE

T. W. Anderson (20)
Lawrence Bengtson (27)
Adelyn Berg (27)
Dan Bergstrom (28)
Curt Bjorlin (29)
Joe Byrne (21)
Isabelle Chryst (22)
Clarice Danielson (21)
Charice Deegan (22)
Geri DeVries (27)
Paul Dwight (21)
Sandy Elhardt (27)
Rich Enderton (29)
Phyllis Englund (22)
E. O. Franklin (22)
Kathy Fretheim (20)
Kenneth Greener (24)
Nancy Greener (21)
Larry Harding (21)
Judith Hinck (23)
F. Justus Hollinbeck (26)
Katie Humason (25)
Kathy Johnson (27)
Lance Johnson (28)
Elwood Lindberg (20)
Sandra Lund (20)
Cynthia McGovern (23)
Ron Monson (22)
Kevin Morris (23)
Roseann Neal (24)
Margaret Nelson (20)

Mary Newhouse (21)
Paul Norby (27)
Mark Norlander (24)
Ezra Oberg (23)
Gordon L. Olson (29)
Karen Olson (24)
Willis Olson (29)
Bev Paulus (21)
Martha Pearson (20)
Bonnie Peterson (21)
Joyce Rottschaefer (21)
Henry Schoultz (22)
Virginia Solvang (24)
Julia Styrlund (24)
Charles Sulack (21)
Evie Swanson (21)
Willamae Swenson (20)
Michelle Breuer Vitt (23)
Karen Wald (29)
Dorothy Wintz (26)

30–39 YEARS OF SERVICE

Arlene Anderson (39)
Ken Anderson (33)
Wally Borner (38)
Mary Carlson (39)
Forrest Dahl (33)
Elaine Ekstedt (39)
Steve Engdahl (30)
Jim Erickson (36)
Phil Erickson (37)
Anna Fellroth (38)

Deb Fondell (31)
Carolyn Forsell (31)
Ruth Francis (31)
Dan Hauge (30)
Gloria Holmen (31)
Paul Isaacs (30)
Carrie Johnson (30)
Janet Johnson (39)
David Lindmark (39)
Theresa Lund (31)
Harvey Lundin (36)
Ted Malmsten (34)
Merry Mattson (33)
Sue McAllister (35)
Bonnie Morris (30)
Sella V. Nelson (31)
Gerald Nordstrom (34)
Harry Opel (37)
Bruce Peterson (30)
Evangeline Peterson (32)
Gertrude Sandberg (32)
Paul Swanson (33)
Diane Thatcher (30)
Renee Troselius (35)

40+ YEARS OF SERVICE

Wendell Carlson (43)
David Glenn (42)
Guido Kauls (44)
Lillian Oberg (41)
Jim Wald (40)

Index

A
Academic Department, 20, 21
Ackerlund-Omark, Marie, 18, 21
Addington, Bonnie, 51
Adell, Joseph R., 38, 40
Ah, Wilderness, 112
Albinson, Pamela, 73
Alumni/Archive House, 7, 116
Alumni Association, Minnehaha. *See* Minnehaha Alumni Association.
Alumni Career Day, 112
Anderson, Arlene, 48
Anderson, Arthur W., 58–59, 121
Anderson, Bonnie, 108
Anderson, David, 3
Anderson, Jeanne, 3
Anderson, Kenneth, 79
Anderson, Theodore W., 18, 19, 23, 25, 27, 29, 30, 33, 40, 120
Anfang, Jane, 23, 45
Antler, 26, 27, 36, 46, 56, 66, 76, 86, 92, 98, 106
Aquatennial, Minneapolis, 73
Arena Sale, 45
Arrow, 30
Athletic Association, Minnehaha. *See* Minnehaha Athletic Association.
Auditorium addition, 64

B
Baccalaureate, 33, 114–115
Bae, Lauren, 109
Band, Minnehaha. *See* Minnehaha Band.
Baseball, 22, 31, 51, 60
Basketball, 23, 31, 41, 51, 52, 53, 60, 82, 102, 111
Beasley, Dan, 93
Benefit Auction and Dinner, 45
Bengston, Dale, 91
Bengtson, Lawrence, 48, 54
Berg, Adelyn, 49
Bergstrom, Dan, 89
Best Blooming Sale Ever, 45
Bestland, Greg, 99
Bethlehem Covenant Church, 19, 54
Bible Institute, 30, 54
Birds of America, 92
Bjorlin, Curt, 90
Bloomdahl, Daniel, 18, 23
Bloomington Campus, 65, 97, 103, 104, 105, 107, 118
Bodin, C. Allan, 78
Borner, Wallace, 80
Bowman, Rev. C. V., 40
Brower, Rebecca, 113
Burns, Joseph E., 18, 19, 21, 23, 27
Buses, 71
Business Department, 19, 31, 37, 64

C
Campus Day, 43
Capel, Ronna, 91
Carlson, Aaron, 10
Carlson, Mary, 79, 82
Carlson, Wendell, 68
Carry On for Christ Campaign, 57
Chapel, 74–75
Cheerleaders, 41
Choral Society, Minnehaha. *See* Minnehaha Choral Society.
Christian Service Club, 61
Christianson, Blake, 104
Christianson, Lorie, 91, 92
Commencement, 114–115
Commercial Department, 20, 21
Community service, 92
Computer, 67, 84, 85
Corps of Collectors, 11, 12, 13
Council of Christian Activities, 42
Covenant Women's Auxiliary, 44
Crafton, Jeffrey, 99
Cross-country running, 81
Cross-country skiing, 92
Culture Fair, 101
Currer, David, 43

D
DaCosta, Courtney (Anderson), 3
Dahl, Forrest, 79, 92
Dahlhielm, Erik, 22, 30
Dance, 55
Danielson, Clarice, 88
Debate, 32, 112
DeVries, Geri, 80
DiNardo, Mike, 99
Dormitory, 117
Dwight, Tim, 113

E
Edquist, P. J., 19, 54
Edmondson, Austin, Jr., 63
Edmondson, William, 52
Ekblad, E. G., 19
Ekstedt, Elaine, 80
Elhardt, Sandy, 90
Enderton, Rich, 85, 88, 113
Engdahl, Steve, 89
Englund, Phyllis M., 49, 62
Engstrom, John B., 97, 98, 104, 107, 123
Environmental Summit Conference, 100
Erickson, Dean, 88, 105
Erickson, James, 69
Erickson, Phillip, 80
Evangelical Covenant Church, 24–25
Evening and Night School, 20, 54

F
Fellowship, Minnehaha. *See* Minnehaha Fellowship.
Fellroth, Anna, 28, 50
Festival of Nations, 101
Fine arts addition, 64, 75
First Covenant Church, Minneapolis, 9, 114
First Covenant Church, St. Paul, 114
Fjelstad, Barb, 108
Florence Nightingale Society, 32
Fondell, Debora, 89, 113
Football, 41, 51, 60
Foote, Lelia, 58, 73
Forsell, Carolyn, 79
Forty Years in Faith, 62
Foundation for a Lifetime Campaign, 65, 107
Francis, Ruth, 90
Franklin, Emanuel O., 38, 40, 50, 120
Franklin, Nathaniel, 18, 19
Fretheim, Kathy, 104

G
George, Ronette, 99
Gilreath, Gayle, 45
Girls' and Boys' State, 52
Girls' Athletic Association, 51
Gjesdahl, Paul G., 49
Glenn, David, 68
Golf, 41
Gospel Team, Minnehaha. *See* Minnehaha Gospel Team.
Graduation, 114–115
Graham, Elliot, 93
Granberg, Gordon, 41
Gravem, Helen Nelson, 54
Greener, Kenneth, 78, 82
Greener, Nancy, 90
Gulden, Janet, 109
Gustafson, Geral, 42
Gustafson, Henry A., 42

H
Hanson, Harlon, 71
Hanson, Marilyn, 53
Harris, Donna M., 6, 107, 108, 123
Harris, Richard, 109
Hauge, Daniel, 89
Hepburn, David, 78, 82
Helping Hands Quarterly, 31, 44
Helping Hands Society, 41
Hockey, 51, 102, 111
Hognander, Marjorie, 1, 42
Hognander, Orville, 1, 42
Holiday House Tour, 110
Hollinbeck, Frank Justus, 28, 92
Holmen, Gloria, 91
Homecoming, 32
Home Economics, 50, 70, 77
Homemaker of Tomorrow, 59
Honor Roll, 32
Humason, Katie, 90

I
Industrial arts, 49, 50, 64, 79
Isaacs, Paul, 88, 109, 113

J
Jaehnert, Larry, 83
Jerde, Peter, 85
Johnson, Carrie, 89
Johnson, Eunice, 53
Johnson, Janet, 78, 82
Johnson, Kathleen, 88
Johnson, Lance, 88
Johnson, Muriel, 42
Johnson, Nancy, 96
Junior High, 83

K
Kauls, Guido, 58, 72, 82, 102, 109
Kindergarten, 78, 93, 102, 116, 118
Kne, Stan, 91
Krueger, Sean, 83

L

Lacrosse, 111
Larose, Mike, 93
Landquist, Alice E. C., 43
Learning Center, 81
Legion, Minnehaha. *See* Minnehaha Legion.
Lettermen's Club, 60
Lindberg, Elwood, 48
Lindblade, J. A., 9
Lindmark, David, 69
Lingua Trainer Language Laboratory, 70
Lower school, 65, 100, 103, 104
Lund, Theresa, 80
Lundin, Harvey, 69, 84

M

"M" Club, 42
MA Alliance, 45
Madrigals, 93
Maeda, Bruce, 108
Magnus, Daniel, 10, 27
Malmsten, Ted, 69
Martinson, Richard, 71
Mascot, 94–95
Matson, Ethel R., 19
Mattson, Merry, 79, 85, 100
McAllister, Sue, 80
McGovern, Cynthia, 90
Melody, 55
Middle school, 111
MILK, 111
MinneAntler, 93
Minneapolis Business School and Bible Institute, The, 9
Minnehaha Alumni Association, 22
Minnehaha Athletic Association, 22
Minnehaha Band, 53
Minnehaha Choral Society, 21
Minnehaha Fellowship, 44
Minnehaha Gospel Team, 42
Minnehaha Legion, 12
Minnehaha Reserves, 11
Minnehaha Singers, 52, 72
Minnehaha Sunday School, 19
Minnesota Independent School Fund, 84
Minnesota Independent School League, 60
Minnesota State High School League, 81
Minnesota State Private School League, 51, 60
Mitlyng, Johnson, 43
Monson, Ronald, 98, 100
Morris, Bonnie, 89, 92
Much Ado About Nothing, 102
Music Department, 18, 21, 23, 26, 38, 49, 64
Music Man, 82

N

Nash, Jim, 7
National Forensic League, 32
National Honor Society, 62
Nelson, Clarence A., 44, 48, 57, 121
Nelson, Craig W., 78, 97, 122
Nelson, Roland, 42
Nelson, Sella V., 28, 59
Noble, Bob, 105
Norby, Paul, 79
Nordstrom, Ethel, 53
Nordstrom, Gerald, 7, 58, 75, 82, 112
North Campus, 13, 65, 87, 97
North Park College, 32, 67
North Park University, 9
Northwest Conference, 24–25, 112, 117
Northwest-Minnehaha Advance Campaign, 47, 57, 64, 74, 118
Northwestern Collegiate and Business Institute, 9
Northwestern Mission Society, 11
Nyvall, David, 9

O

Oberg, Ezra N., 19
Oberg, Lillian, 19
Olson, Barb, 78
Olson, Gordon L., 68, 92
Olson, Gordon R., 88, 92, 99
Olson, Willis, 58
Opel, Bonnevieve, 91
Opel, Harry P., 49, 82, 91
Osterberg, Cecil, 43
Osterlund, Paul, 88

P

Palmquist, A. Eldon, 68
Parents and Teachers Association, 14, 52
Pearson, Martha, 48
Pearson, Robert N., 38, 42, 53
Peterson, Betty, 53
Peterson, Bruce, 91
Peterson, Evangeline, 49
Peterson, Janet, 90
Peterson, Joel S., 37, 38, 40
Prayer Chapel, 72
Preparatory Department, 21, 29, 38
Promise for the Future Campaign, 65, 107

Q

Quiggle, Milton, 53
Quill, 36
Quill Club, 37
Quiver, 27, 30, 39, 92, 94–95, 100, 102

R

Ramierez, Homar, 108
Redhawks, 35, 94-95
Redhawksonline.com, 85
Reedholm, Ruth, 50
Reserves, Minnehaha. *See* Minnehaha Reserves.
River Project, 105
River Road, 10, 14, 34
Rock-a-Thon, 82
Roll of Honor, 13

S

Sadie Hawkins, 55, 72
Sandberg, Gertrude, 28, 59, 62
Sandberg, Lillian, 38
Sandin, Zella Mae, 55, 62
Scandinavian Holiday Festival, 110
Scholl, Scott, 98
School Song, 23
Schoultz, Henry, 28, 43
Sedgwick, Flora, 68
Serve It Day, 105
Silver Jubilee Campaign, 41
Simso, Amy, 93
Singers, Minnehaha. *See* Minnehaha Singers.
Skogsbergh, Erik August, 8, 9, 27
Skoog, Andrew L., 11, 12, 13, 23, 34, 64
Snow Day, 52
Soccer, 67, 72, 101
Softball, 31, 41, 111
Solvang, Virginia, 69, 100
Sonlight, 111
Sorenson, Ann, 98
South Campus, 65, 75, 85, 87, 93, 97, 118
Spirit, 82, 83, 92, 93
Spiritual Life Committe, 111
Stone, Sara, 109
Strandberg, Arlene, 53
Strandberg, John, 28
Student Athletic Board, 31
Student Council, 22, 61
Student Diversity Club, 101
Student Intern Program, 110
Sulack, Charles, 49, 50
Summer School, 93
Sunday School, Minnehaha. *See* Minnehaha Sunday School.
Swanson, Evelyn, 80
Swanson, Paul, 69
Swedish, 8, 9, 11, 22, 33, 54
Swedish Tabernacle, 9, 114
Swenson, Lorraine, 42
Swenson, Willamae, 90
Swimming, 102, 111

T

Talon, 102
Tennis, 41, 81
Tewinkel, Kristen, 104
Thatcher, Diane, 91
Thousand Tens Campaign, 17, 64
Todhunter, Paulita, 108
Track, 31, 51, 81
Tri-Metro Conference, 81, 101
Troselius, Renee, 80
Twin City Academic League, 31

U

Universal Sign Company, 15
Upper school, 110

V

Veckobladet, 8, 22
Volleyball, 41, 81

W

Wald, James, 79
Wald, Karen, 89
Wallentine, Gordon, 14
Wallentine, Margaret, 14
Wallentine, Stanley, 14
Wedell, Axel Leonard, 19
Westerdahl, Wilbur M., 68, 77, 122
Where Youth Meets Truth, 7, 25, 112
Williamson, Lance, 91
Wintz, Dorothy, 90
Women's Committee, 45
Wrestling, 60, 89, 111, 112

Bibliography

BOOKS

Anderson, Philip J. *A Precious Heritage: A Century of Mission in the Northwest, 1884–1984.* Minneapolis, Minnesota: Northwest Conference, 1984.

Anderson, Theodore W. "Minnehaha Academy's Early Years," *Covenant Companion*, Vol. LIII, No. 19 (May 8, 1964).

Englund, Phyllis M. and Gertrude A. Sandberg. *Forty Years in Faith: A Brief History of Minnehaha Academy, 1913–1953.* Minneapolis, Minnesota: privately published, 1953.

Nelson, Craig W. "Rooted and Growing," *Covenant Companion* (September 1, 1983).

Nordstrom, Gerald T. *Where Youth Meets Truth: A History of Minnehaha Academy.* Minneapolis, Minnesota: Minnehaha Academy, 2001.

ARCHIVE MATERIALS

In addition to the works listed in the Bibliography, the majority of information was provided through research of original materials available in the Minnehaha Academy archives.

UNPUBLISHED SCHOOL MATERIAL

- School Board meeting minutes
- Board of Education minutes
- Faculty meeting minutes
- Personal correspondence
- Personal scrapbooks

MINNEHAHA PUBLICATIONS
INSTITUTIONAL PUBLICATIONS

- Minnehaha Academy Catalogs and Viewbooks
- Annual Reports
- School brochures and event programs
- *Minnehaha Academy News*
- *The Academy News*
- *The Alumnus*
- *Arrow*

STUDENT PUBLICATIONS

- *Antler* yearbook
- *Quill*
- *Quiver* newspaper
- *Talon* newspaper

SCHOOL WEBSITES

- MinnehahaAcademy.net
- redhawksonline.com